W9-ATN-461

# Experiments in Prayer

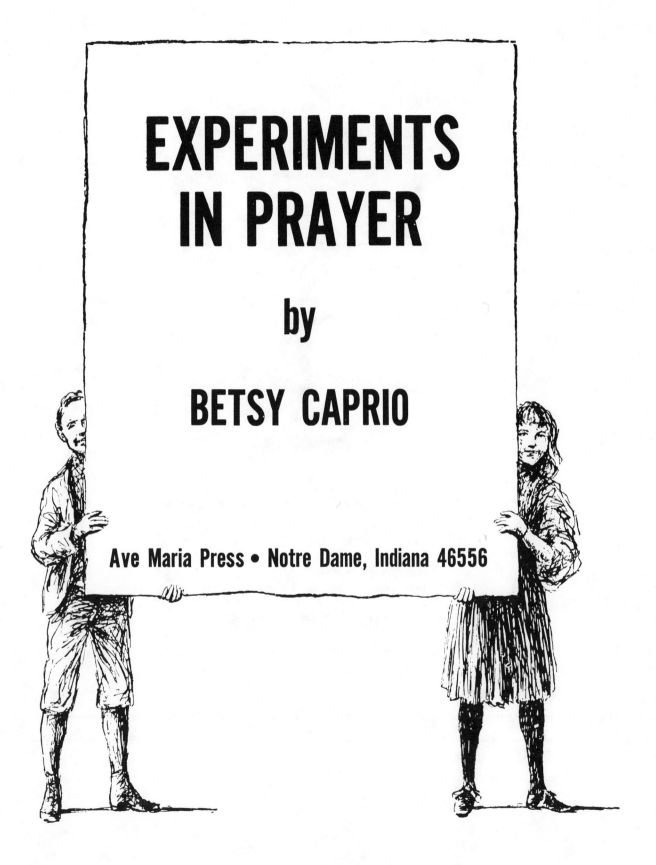

# EXPERIMENTS IN PRAYER

## by

## BETSY CAPRIO

Ave Maria Press • Notre Dame, Indiana 46556

International Standard Book Number: 0-87793-054-6

© 1973 by Ave Maria Press. All rights reserved

First printing, May, 1973
Fourth printing, February, 1978
40,000 copies in print.

Design and layout: *Charles E. Jones* and
                   *Anthony F. Rowland*

Printed in the United States of America

# CONTENTS

# THE PRAYER EXPERIMENTS

# INTRODUCTION

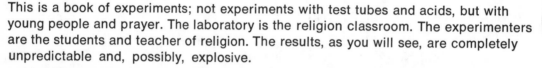

This is a book of experiments; not experiments with test tubes and acids, but with young people and prayer. The laboratory is the religion classroom. The experimenters are the students and teacher of religion. The results, as you will see, are completely unpredictable and, possibly, explosive.

I began this book as a collection of ideas for myself, hoping it would lead my own students beyond our routine prayer times which bored them silly. It grew, like a healthy plant, fertilized by ideas from the young-in-years and the young-in-heart. The thoughts in this book ought to continue to sprout, as other teachers read it and say, "Well, this experiment wouldn't be so great for my class, but it gives me an even better idea. . . ." I hope it will be a catalyst.

Though the experiments grew out of classes with junior high students, they're suitable with slight adjustments for all age groups and some would, I think, be of value for private prayer as well. And while the soil these ideas sprang from was Roman Catholic, only a few suggestions are exclusively Christian. Most can easily be adapted by believers of any faith.

Readers will sense a lightheartedness in many of the experiments. This matches the mood of most religion students, who generally are not panting in anticipation of their catechizing (especially if they come to us after a full day of school or on weekends). Far more important, however, this light touch also echoes the mood of the Good News, the happy mood of celebration upon learning how much God loves us all.

The experiments divide into three groups, following a pair of chapters discussing classroom prayer in general. The first group of experiments is based on traditional ways of praying in schools: memorized prayers, prayers written by someone else and read, and spontaneous prayers. These are always valid and good, and can be varied in a few ways; however, by themselves, these garden-variety prayers can become so routine and tedious as to convince even the most open student that praying is about as important as deciding whether to pick up pizza or sloppy joes in the cafeteria.

A second group of experiments rings changes on those standbys of all classrooms: small groups, pencil and paper activities, and music. Finally, a collection of 20 experiments goes beyond the usual sort of student-teacher praying, creating "settings" for moments of prayer—I guess this makes them happenings. The last of these is a giant one- or two-hour prayer experiment, for classes that really are sparkling.

Not all the experiments will work for all students, of course, but all will work for some students—and help them tune in, get in touch with, and (hopefully) love more the God who transforms lives. A plan for making the best use of the prayer experiments is suggested in Chapter 2.

Many sources led to the ideas in this book, for praying has been going on from the day man realized there was a Someone larger than himself. Some are techniques in current use all over the world; it is hoped that the collecting of them will be a service to other teachers. I have tried to give credit wherever I could and I apologize if I've neglected to mention anyone whose similar work may have appeared in print before. The meditations, and many other experiments, are original plans from my own classrooms, although they clearly have their roots in varied sources. All the experiments have been worked out with and tested by my own students with success —and fun.

I haven't included any experiments or ideas on liturgical prayer, as that is really beyond the scope of this work. However, prayer is prayer, and we can reasonably hope that the young person who has been helped to be more aware of God through classroom experiments in personal prayer will find there is a carry-over to his appreciation of public prayer. Obviously, also, many of the activities in the prayer experiments can be divorced from praying and used for other classroom purposes.

Certainly, I must thank several people who helped precipitate this book. Lots of good sharing came from my fellow faculty members at St. Teresa's Church in Pittsfield, Massachusetts, especially Father Tom Lefebvre, Elaine Broderick and Bob Esposito. At this fortunate parish, the pastor, Father John P. Lucey, and the religious education coordinator, Sister Jacinta Jurasek, R.S.M., have created a climate of freedom which makes experimenting not only possible but also lots of fun.

Chief thanks should go to my own children and my students, who were "subjects" for the prayer experiments and were nothing if not honest with their opinions (as in "Gee, Mom, what a rotten idea. You're not going to make the poor kids in your class do *that,* are you?"). Their sureness for what works and what is hopelessly square was my touchstone! Special help was given by three students, who deserve extra thanks— Timothy Douglas, Bruce Gionet and David Vayo.

I would be delighted to see any original experiments which readers may dream up. Perhaps they can someday be recycled.

# chapter 1
# PRAYER IN THE CLASSROOM

*Concerned Mother:* "What did you do in religion class today, dear?"

*Twelve-year-old Andy:* "Well, the teacher heard Cecelia call him 'Mr. Cool' and Chris and Brian had a fight and . . . ."

*C.M.:* "But how about your lesson? What was that about?"

*Andy:* "Oh yeah, we learned about the guys who wrote the gospels."

*C.M.:* (moving in) "How interesting. Who were they?"

*Andy:* "I don't know. What's for supper?"

And so on. We could each flesh out this dialogue, perhaps even bringing Andy to the concession that he knew the names of the evangelists and had some idea of how their writing turned the world upside down. But even if Andy, and Cecelia, and Brian, and Chris, and everyone in their class are each well informed about the New Testament—and about the Church, the sacraments and so forth—will they really be "religiously educated"? How long will they remember what they learn about Matthew, Mark and Luke, to say nothing of John? More important, will remembering make them living, overflowing Christians?

The question of the goal of religious education has been argued endlessly. Although most of us have moved away from traditional catechisms, our texts are still largely information-centered. Although we have moved into a new world of activity in the classroom, with teachers up to their whiskers in projectors, tape recorders, slides and art supplies, still the purpose of these tools usually is to relay information *about* God and man to the students—or, better still, help them uncover this information for themselves.

Surely it is good for teachers to relay information to students. And yet, if this is all we are doing, then isn't it possible that these same students may leave us, after a whole year of classes, knowing *about* God but still not *knowing* God? There is a difference. If they spend eight to 12 years in religion classes, never (well, hardly ever)

actually encountering God, can we be so surprised if they don't feel very excited about him as adults?

"But they do encounter God," some of us would say. "The information we give them (with all our multimedia techniques) helps them to know him and therefore love him." Possibly. "And what's more, we pray with them." Yes, we do, and the God we pray to surely knows we try to pray sincerely, even beautifully. The question is, however, do our classroom prayers help anyone to be touched by the experience of God? Shouldn't this, the experience of God, really be the main focus of religious education?

If our students don't experience the divine, "taste the Lord" as the psalm says, will all their information about him help them to love him from the bottom of their hearts? Can anyone ever be on fire with the love of God with just knowledge for fuel —or mustn't he also be acutely aware of the presence of God through having experienced him?

Since prayer is the means we have of coming in touch with God, of having this experience of him and his presence, then religion teachers might take a second look at what's going on in their classes under the name of prayer. Eavesdropping on many a religion classroom might reveal excellent teachers who were somewhat short of inspiring when it came to "prayer time." "Now everyone, let's stand and pray: 'In the name of the Father' . . ." may be the signal for real communication with God, but it very possibly is a ritual with about as much meaning as "Collect your books, zip up and line up."

Or, do we hear this as we continue our spying? "Who has a prayer for us today?" (Darkness there and nothing more.) "No one? All right then, Lucy, please read the prayer in lesson 14 and, Helen, please stop talking. Excuse me, Lucy . . . just a minute now. Tom, come up front, and, Sue, please pay attention . . . doesn't anyone *want* to talk to God today?" (Let's leave before the kids answer that one.)

What would honest answers to questions like these bring from our students?

- When we pray together do you feel that you have made an effort to reach God?

- Do you feel that you have made it possible for him to reach you?

- Is prayer time a big, fat drag for you?

- Has your life been changed by prayer time in this class?

If lives are not being changed by prayers in the classroom, if these prayer times are not producing honest and moving encounters between young people and their God, and if we believe that this experiential knowledge of God is the most valuable sort of religious learning, then we must begin to try to make each prayer time "contact time" with the Lord.

## WHAT CAN WE DO?

Education is being revolutionized, slowly, by teachers and psychologists like Carl Rogers, who reiterate the ancient truth that what man learns through experience, he truly makes his own (see Rogers' *Freedom to Learn.* Columbus, Ohio: Charles E. Merrill Pub. Co., 1969. $7.50). Or, put another way, that affective learning (based on feeling) plus cognitive learning (based on thinking) is better than cognitive alone. Religious educators have taken this message to heart, and teachers' manuals from textbook publishers are full of good ideas on how to facilitate self-learning in the student. Now, have we done as much to apply the principle of learning through experiencing to prayer itself (which should be the experience of experiences) as we have to learning about the bible, the life of Jesus, and all our many other topics?

If not, what can we do to improve and bring alive classroom prayer? Two answers are suggested in this book: first, giving a greater weight to the prayer time of a class; and, second, devising somewhat more elaborate settings for prayer than we usually offer our students. These settings are called "prayer experiments." Before describing them, we should take a closer look at the most basic question of all, which is

## WHAT IS PRAYER?

The traditional catechism definition, still very fine, is "the raising of the heart and mind to God." Religion teachers might elaborate a little, and come up with a working definition of prayer along the lines of the following:

Prayer is contact with God, which may come through

1) our attempts at communication with him and/or

2) his communication with us.

Then we might add that in order to receive God's communications (2), we must be receptive, aware, tuned in, quieted. Our students are familiar with the contact which comes through their own reaching out (1), but usually much less at home with the idea of God speaking as they open their souls to him (2). Perhaps they think he speaks only with burning bushes and thunderbolts, Hollywood-style. Perhaps they have never been told about the "still, small voice" of God.

Some readers will say that we are describing contemplative prayer, the prayer of the saints, and that spiritual writers have often advised against seeking this great gift. True. There's a distinction, however, between actively seeking this awareness of God and laying ourselves open *to receive it* if he wants to send this blessing. The argument as to whether or not contemplative prayer is suitable to the active life has long since been buried; the question today hinges on whether or not the young can and should be introduced to an understanding of higher prayer.

We might ask whether so many young Americans would now be fascinated by (and following) the religions of the East had they been introduced to the rich contemplative heritage of Christianity during their own religious educations. How many of these young people know that the "cosmic consciousness" which makes Hinduism and Buddhism (as well as drugs and the occult) so attractive is also the result of Christian prayer? Did they ever hear from us, their religion teachers, what they have learned from Eastern sources: that the interior life of a whole man is life's most intoxicating high, the peak experience (to borrow Abraham Maslow's expression)?

Why can't we develop for our young people the romance with mystery (rather than with intellectualism) so many sense at the core of the Asian faiths? It's part of their tradition as Christians.

True, we are seeing some wonderful outbursts of faith among young people in our time, but most of these occur *after* they've been through formal religious education and have been turned off beautifully by the established churches. If, from the time our students entered a church school, they were helped to prepare themselves for whatever awareness of God he wants to send them, surely their lives would be richer. They will discover soon enough, as we have, that God comes only when and where he pleases—but all of us can, at the very least, be ready and open should he please.

The higher forms of prayer are the Church's "pearl of great price." Most religion students never hear of them at all.

## THE PRAYER EXPERIMENTS

The experiments in this book make use of both parts of our definition of prayer. Some are simple attempts to reach out and communicate with God; others are attempts, more complicated, to make ourselves open to "the religious experience," with no preconceptions or promises about what will happen if we succeed. This is up to God.

Each experiment includes some activity which leads up to a key point, the point of turning the heart and mind to God. For most students, this will probably be a matter of a few seconds per experiment, if at all. Some experiments are prayers of petition, some of thanksgiving or praise, others of sorrow. Some are just "Here I am, Lord" prayers.

The word "unpredictable" is important in connection with classroom praying, for there certainly is no magic answer as to what sort of praying will work. What works for Mary Louise may turn Mike off completely, and the form of prayer that hits Sarah just right in September may be unusable, for her, in May. By offering our students a wide variety of ways to "connect" with God, however, we're pretty sure to help all of them reach him at least a few times during the year. And by giving prayer a more interesting format in our classes, we can hope to help each student (and the teacher) expand his awareness of the spiritual, a lifelong project.

It's a start.

Need Help?

# THINK!

## chapter 2
## SOME FOOD
## FOR THOUGHT

In order to make classroom prayer the means for growth that it might be, we may have to do some rethinking. Let's start by examining the ingredients of prayer in an educational setting.

### THE TEACHER

As education writers never tire of saying, the teacher is the must ingredient in successful education; this is doubly true of the teacher who is also a pray-er. Until we ourselves have two very vital qualities, we probably won't have the results we hope for in praying with our students. We must, first, be true men and women of prayer and, second, we must be completely convinced that young people can and will grow through prayer. These qualifications sound so obvious for a religion teacher, yet they are often the biggest hurdle to overcome.

Most of us would like to think we are "true men and women of prayer," but this means being someone who constantly finds God in the people and things around him, someone who is rounded and keeps in touch with God all through the day. The person whose life is deeply (not just "sort of") prayer-full doesn't lose sight of God when a dozen little problems have to be solved at once (this is the author's Waterloo). The man or woman to whom praying is daily bread has a sureness, a naturalness when he prays that students pick up on their ever-alert antennae. The teacher, on the other hand, whose own prayer life is mechanical and bland, cranked out, sends out one big neon-lit message before a class of students he has asked to pray: PHONY.

Some teachers have a rich personal prayer life, yet still find it hard to pray easily before a group of students (especially if Jack the Ripper, Jr., 15, in his black leather jacket is sneering from the back row). They can loosen up by getting in touch with good pray-ers. Most towns have Sunday radio or TV programs featuring evangelists who talk up a storm with the Lord. Many areas have prayer groups of Pentecostal Christians, who are part of the whole charismatic renewal. Making a cursillo brings one in touch with some no-nonsense praying, and just shopping around among the local clergy on Sunday mornings (and other times) can unearth a few men in each community who seem especially plugged in to God. Being with such people rubs off on even the shyest teacher after a while, and what once seemed abnormal—that is, to stand before 20-odd other people and talk to God—can soon become the most authentic thing in one's world.

The second essential quality a teacher will need to pray successfully with his class, namely, the conviction that praying will help change his students' lives for the better, follows on the first. As we sense what our own improving prayer life is doing for us, we know with our hearts as well as our heads that this is the direct route to spiritual growth for other people too. Something in us says, "Yes, this is good; it rings true." And then something in almost all students will say, "Yes, my teacher has something good; it rings true." We will have become more than a warm body in front of a class.

Somewhere around this stage, we can begin to hope that experiments in prayer will get off the ground and start to take wing.

## SETTING THE STAGE

As with any experiment, some preparation has to be made before one actually begins. In spite of the good efforts of many wonderful religion teachers, the majority of our students probably aren't kicking up their heels at the thought of praying with the rest of the class. To lay some sort of groundwork for what we hope to do, at the beginning of the year a class should be told the teacher's ideas on the value of prayer and the students' ideas on the subject should be probed. Discussions are good, although sometimes on personal matters like this (especially with older students) an anonymous questionnaire (not necessarily mimeod) is even better. If you try this you might ask questions like:

- How often do you pray? Why do you do it?

- Do you have a definite time to pray each day?

- Do you have a special place to pray?

- Do you use prayers you've memorized or do you make up your own?

- If an atheist asked you to give him one good reason for praying, what would you say?

- Do you think you're mature enough to do some experimenting in prayer this year?

This last question, of course, might come under both the heading of setting the stage and of conning the kids (and where is the successful teacher who is not part con artist?). Unsigned answers to questions like these are often more frank than spoken answers, and this method also gives the quiet students a chance to be heard.

Assuming that the teacher hasn't become totally discouraged at this point by 25 answer papers that say "I hate to pray," "Drop dead, lady" and feedback of that sort, the next suggestion is to build up the prayer time that will be a regular feature of each class. If praying is, indeed, the most valuable thing we can do with religion students, then the time for it (only a few minutes) deserves to have the place of honor. A regular time slot in each class is important: Some teachers like to begin with prayer to set the tone for the whole class; others prefer to get announcements, homework and quizzes out of the way before praying. Sandwiching the prayer time in between the little "bits and pieces," however, or saving it until the end of class are both inadvisable.

The teacher should also let his students know how he feels about prayer—and this can be very easy or murderously hard, depending on what sort of faces are looking back at you from across the crowded room. (More on difficult classes later.) But no matter what sort of class he faces, the teacher who is a person of prayer and believes in the power of prayer must tell his class this. Has he examples of the "wonders wrought by prayer" from his own experience: changed lives, little everyday miracles? He should tell them. Has he ever been given the strength to face an impossible situation (his first religion class?) by God's answer to his prayers? He should tell them. Do the students know of any good results of prayer, either in their own lives, or in the lives of others? Do they know any of the saint stories (yes, saints, even today) that make the power of prayer come alive? (St. Catherine of Siena and the Cure of Ars spring to mind, among many others.)

Do they know what Jesus said about prayer? Are there individual bibles so that each can look up his words on the subject? If not, the students might take turns reading and discussing these verses from the classroom bible:

. . . when you pray, go to your room and close the door, and pray to your Father, who is unseen. And your Father, who sees what you do in private, will reward you. (Mt 6:6)

. . . the Father will give you anything you ask of him in my name . . . ask and you will receive, so that your happiness may be complete. (Jn 16:23-24)

Other verses show the importance of prayer to Jesus in his life, telling of how he was up before daylight to pray (Mk 1: 35), how he prayed all night (Lk 6: 12), how he prayed for others (Jn 17), and especially how he prayed when he most needed help (Mt 26: 36-44; Lk 23: 34 and 46).

Let's face it, with some boys and girls the only motivation which works will be an answer to "What's in it for me?" And so, we tell them. What's in praying for them is help when there's no one else to help you, love when there's no one else to love you, and (would they believe?), for eternity, happiness beyond belief.

Hopefully, by this time the atmosphere for praying has mellowed. The class can be told your intentions, to set aside a small time weekly (or daily, if that's the case) for experiments to see if they and you, the teacher, can grow in prayer. You can mention that you hope to try many sorts of prayers with them, and that the limits to which you can go will be determined only by the maturity of the students. They should understand that the goal all are aiming for is a closer personal relation-

ship with God, based on a variety of ways of reaching him.

Important also is the idea that whatever is done in class prayer time will be strictly between each person and God. Prayer time shouldn't be crawl-under-the-desk time because Mrs. Grommet has asked someone to strip his soul in public. While volunteers and comments are most appreciated, no one should ever be called on to pray or forced to pray out loud. Whatever private thoughts occur during prayer time are exactly that—private. They should be respected as such, and the students should be aware of this nonthreatening atmosphere so they can give themselves to praying, not to preparing an answer in case the teacher pounces on them with, "Now Julie, what did *you* say to God?"

This preparation before the actual experiments begin can be spread over two or three weeks. Reading this, it may sound time-consuming but actually both the preparation and all the experiments except the last one take only a few minutes of each class.

## USING THE PRAYER EXPERIMENTS

Before the first experiment, the whole idea should be given a final buildup to create an atmosphere of "Here we go, into an unknown venture together . . . who knows how far we can go?" We should ask for, and *wait* for, perfect attention. Nothing is worse than prayer plus chitchat between a couple of students on the side. Remind the class that God is with them in the classroom, as he is everywhere, and that if prayer is really as important as we've been saying it is then it deserves to be done splendidly. Then start, using whichever of the many prayer experiments in this book strikes you as just right for your particular class. Or, better still, make up your own.

For some groups, a simple and familiar sort of prayer is best for openers, with the promise of more elaborate things to come. For others, especially an alert and creative bunch, the "fancy" prayer settings might best capture their attention and curiosity. (The author's own favorite for a first prayer experiment, at least with junior and senior high students, is the "This Is Your Life" Meditation, Experiment No. 33—*if* the subject of death is not too close to home for anyone in the class. Schools with permanent records will give you this information.) Here, as in so many other aspects of teaching, the teacher's intuition as to what is best is the thing to go on.

Perhaps you will want to choose a type of prayer that ties in with the subject you're teaching that day; this is desirable, of course, but not essential. Prayer time should—and can—stand on its own. Connection of subject matter between the prayer time and the regular lesson is helpful (see the Index), but an even more useful guideline for choosing an experiment is that the type of prayer should be varied from class to class. A musical prayer one period could be followed next time with something completely different, like a group prayer, and so on. Also, repeating the same experiment a few months later, if it has gone well, isn't a bad idea.

There are days when the simplest possible prayer will be the best, due to the nature of your lesson, the mood of the class or events in a student's family, the community or the world at that time. For example, a death in the family of a student might seem to call for a moment of silent prayer or a prayer to some quiet music, rather than anything more elaborate or fanciful.

The most tricky sort of praying to pull off is that in which students are asked to speak. Save these until you really get the prayer time rolling, unless you are blessed with a vocal and uninhibited class. If you do have many students who pray freely before others, without embarrassment, you are probably part of a five percent minority of religion teachers in America and greatly to be envied by the rest of us. Let us know your secret.

If the students have notebooks, and if there is time, another idea is to have them keep a log of the prayer experiments. It could look like this:

*date* | *prayer experiment* | *results* | *follow-up*

After each experiment students can put the information in their notebooks and eventually have a collection of ideas for prayer along with thoughts on what works best for them. You will want to point out that, although something tried in class may seem utterly useless just now to some people each time, in a few years—or 30 years—it may be just the sort of prayer style Al or Janet will need. A record like this will help young people remember the many approaches to God, both for present and future reference. If we each have the obligation to make the most of our human potential, then we have a responsibility to keep trying all sorts of ways to help our souls develop. Prayer is the best way to do this, and growing in prayer is the work of a lifetime.

Whether or not logs are kept, you might follow up each experiment with the suggestion that students try the experiment again at home during the coming week. If it doesn't work for them, they should feel free to forget it, or, better still, tuck the idea away in some spare cranny of their heads for future reference.

Offer, too, to allow students to run prayer time, presenting their own experiments (after first clearing their ideas with you). Often, their knowledge of each other and their feel for the pulse of their world will help create far better experiments than any teacher-inspired praying.

## HOW THE EXPERIMENTS ARE SET UP

Each of the "lab pages" in this book is divided into four sections. The top portion has suggestions about background and vocabulary the teacher may want to cover with the class or put on the board before starting, materials to assemble, possible tie-ins to religion curriculum topics and immediate preparation of the class. The word "usual" under the heading *Preparation of Class* means these four things:

• Announce prayer time.

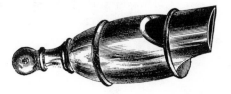

- Wait for silence and calm.

- Remind the students that whatever happens between themselves and God, who is always present with them, won't have to be revealed to anyone else.

- Invite everyone to join in (leaving the option up to each student).

The left side of the body of each experiment is a *suggested* script for the teacher. Obviously, it is not necessary or even a good idea to read these verbatim; teachers will want to ad lib their own language and examples in whatever way is most real for them and for their classes. With experience, teachers develop interesting voices (we hope), so that students are spared listening to a never-ending, droning monotone. Check your voice for expression against that of a good TV or radio announcer, or on a tape recorder, to see if your presentation of a prayer experiment is blah or catching.

The dots (. . .) indicate a pause, giving students and you time to think of what you've been saying. If your class is keeping a log, or if you want to suggest that students try a prayer experiment again at home, you can add a note to that effect at the end of the left-hand column.

The right side of each experiment page contains suggestions and "stage directions," and leaves open space for the teacher to fill in his own ideas as he goes along.

The final section of each experiment, at the bottom, has blank space for the teacher's notes on the date tried and the length of time used (which may vary from class to class), a space for a decision on whether or not to repeat the experiment, and for notes on how it went (results). A minute taken after class to fill in this information will give a helpful record for future years.

## PROBLEMS WITH CLASSROOM PRAYER

Many teachers feel that a classroom, by its very nature, is the most unreal place possible to ask anyone to pray. For most boys and girls, classrooms represent hard work, subjection to authority and judgment, and physical restraint. These are just the opposite of the atmosphere necessary for loving communication with God. To pray, one should feel relaxed, free and at ease. Can we do anything to make the average religion classroom less heavy?

This question brings us right back to the religion teacher and his or her very personality. Despite the fact that we have to be authority figures in order to have order in our classrooms, despite the fact that we are involved in an academic situation and must uphold standards of academic excellence, the key fact remains that the religion teacher should be a breed apart. If our students were asked to honestly describe us in one word, we must hope the first thoughts to pop into their heads would be words like "kind," "caring," "concerned," and other such happy syllables.

The person of the teacher is the greatest factor in religious education, and in the tone of the classroom; the empathetic and un-self-centered teacher who deeply cares about his students goes a long way to making the religion classroom a relaxed and easy place in which to pray.

Depending upon where we teach, there may or may not be things we can do to make our classrooms look homey and inviting. Teachers have transformed drab spaces into new worlds for hundreds of years with pictures, banners, posters, mobiles, real furniture, dividers, music, cartoons, different furniture arrangements, plants, refreshments and dozens of other kind things. One of the most popular devices, and easiest, for creating atmosphere is the use of candles. Evening classes, which can turn out the lights and have prayer time by candlelight, are fortunate, but candles during the day have a magic too and help set a tone of reverence with students of all ages. They are special; they are churchy; they work. Try them. (*You* light them.)

Some teachers vary their environment by meeting occasionally in different parts of their buildings, or outdoors if it's nice. Outdoor prayer—and classes—can be especially fine, if your class is pretty well behaved. More than a few churches have cellar rooms not unlike the catacombs, both in age and dismalness—these might be a spot for a prayer experiment like No. 27, the Early Christians' Meditation. For a prayer about Baptism, why not pray at the baptismal font in church? Once we start thinking along these lines, from a student's viewpoint, we find we can do a good bit toward creating what the Montessori schools call a "prepared environment."

Another problem to conquer, or at least tackle, is the stiffness so many young people feel about prayer in general. If prayers can be said in a natural, intimate way, without all the rubrics of standing, folding of hands, blessing of selves (for Catholic and Orthodox pray-ers), and all sorts of catch phrases that are really cliches, they become more human. No law was ever handed down from Mount Sinai, or anywhere else, saying that man, in talking to God, has to suddenly stiffen up as though he had swallowed an Easter candle. And Jesus himself tells us ". . . . do not use a lot of words (in your prayers), as the pagans do, who think that God will hear them because of their long prayers" (Mt 6: 7).

It's not that ritual prayer and the trimmings of formal worship aren't usable even in classrooms, but there's no need to impose them on young people who very much need and will respond to down-to-earth praying. The solemnity of church worship is often the only sort of prayer young people know, because their teachers and parents have used only paraliturgical styles of prayer in school and at home. We can let them relax with God. If our young people understand the concept of respect for the One with whom they're communicating, posture and format of prayer become secondary. A religion class should be one place, certainly, where (to quote the late Frederick S. Perls) "there's some beautiful melting going on."

A third problem facing praying teachers and students is the perpetual problem of discipline. We know that preventive discipline is the best sort and that we achieve this in our classrooms in two ways. The first and major factor is, again,

23

the teacher and who he or she really is. The teacher sure of what he's doing, why he's doing it, and what his standards are (or the teacher who can *act* sure until he is!) has already taken care of almost all discipline problems just by radiating sureness. Then, too, many problems are prevented by frequent reminders to the students of what our standards are *before* they've had a chance to forget them. Therefore, ever so often, even at each class, a reminder is in order about why we're praying, about the necessity for taking this time seriously, about the experimental, open-ended quality of the prayer time and the variety of reactions possible with each experiment, or about our own confidence in our students' maturity in prayer (ah, what faith!).

And, to repeat, a minimum and an absolute must before beginning every prayer experiment is to ask for, and wait for, complete attention and silence.

Most discipline troubles are taken care of by these measures, but there are always those times. . .

. . . when restlessness just fills the air, usually the class before Christmas vacation or the first nice day of spring. Skip the prayer rather than not do it really well—and tell the class why.

. . . when a prayer which starts off well is upset by someone who was hit by a hilarious thought at the wrong time. Look shocked, even horrified; perhaps say, "Oh Jim, how could you let us down?" If Jim's still beside himself, stop and tell the class you value prayer too much to offer God less than the best. Tell them you'll try again next week. Keep Jim after class for a "little talk" and nail him! Make him an offer he can't refuse. . .

. . . when some really tough kid makes his disgust with this goody-goody stuff all too obvious. Ask him to wait in the hall until prayer time is over and hope he won't run away. After class tell him that since your last purpose is to force prayer on anyone who doesn't come to it freely, out of faith (as if we could), he has a choice: He can sit quietly during prayer time, perfectly free not to participate but not disturbing anyone who wants to, or he can be excused from class for the few minutes prayers take each period. Start praying for him yourself.

This leads us to the occasional teacher in the difficult position of teaching almost an entire class of very rough boys and girls, those who seem to live by the law of the jungle. Can this teacher even hope to begin to pray with kids carrying switchblades in their pockets and armadillo-thick shells over their hearts? Or should he drop the whole thing?

Most of us might say "Forget it," until we stop to realize that these boys and girls are the very ones most in need of God in their lives. Often growing up with fierce home problems and poverty, they—far more than our polite, if giddy, middle-class students—need desperately to believe that God loves and will stand by them. (Maybe there's no one else who will.) They may not know this yet, and probably would not admit it did they know. Somehow, some way, they're here in a classroom, ours for one hour. Now what?

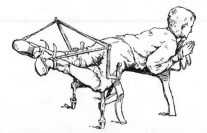

Let's first assume that no teacher would be in this role in the first place unless he or she had a lot of inner strength (which the kids can read loud and clear), and let's also assume that this teacher has firm convictions about the value of prayer, which he is willing to share with his captive audience. Perhaps the best tack he can take is to play it by ear, throwing out all rules while still keeping the goals of a fruitful prayer time in mind.

For starters, he might (after telling his class why he believes in praying) ask the class to let him pray for them. If they will respect his wishes and be quiet for even 15 seconds, he can make up something like this.

"Lord, here we are, some of your children. All of us need help and we know you're the only one who can give it to us. So, please help us. Amen."

Maybe, possibly, after a few weeks of carrying the prayer time himself, asking nothing of his class but silence, the teacher will be able to move on to something else which requires no commitment on the part of the students (like reading prayers—Malcolm Boyd's books are good, or listening to a song that can also be a prayer). After that, his hunches must be his guide.

One thing is sure (in a world where not a great deal is), the inner strength and peace of a man or woman who is trying to stay close to God shines from him— Paul tells the Philippians (2:15) and us to "shine in the world like bright stars"— and has a power to reach and change even the toughest boys and girls. The teacher may never know that this has happened, but it does, and often. The books of David Wilkerson, especially *The Cross and the Switchblade* (New York: Pyramid Books, 1964. 95 cents), offer lots of hope for teachers working with such students.

Maddeningly enough, there's also the problem of the apathetic class, the one where you could swear everyone was either half-stoned or dying of sleeping sickness. An occasional student in a class like this may come out of her trance-like state to roll (heavily made-up) eyes at another, indicating her conviction that you must surely be advancing rapidly into the last stages of senility. If you can overcome the acute desire to go around the room and shake everyone, you may wonder whether or not a prayer time here can ever get off the ground.

Perhaps the best thing with the sophisticates is a bombshell, something to really shake them up. The "This Is Your Life" experiments (Nos. 26, 33, and 39) might do it, if you dwell on the death scene a little: Describe the satin-lined coffins, the pallor of the corpses (them!). Or the Early Christians' Meditation (No. 27) could meet a decidedly grisly fate, if you think this might get a rise out of such a class. (Yes, you'd *like* to find some lions to turn loose on them, with yourself as Nero or Diocletian.)

And, although no one should ever be forced to pray, you can ask them to participate in an activity leading to prayer, such as anonymously writing down their problems (Experiment No. 19, Advice Clinic). Kids like this are usually big on one subject—themselves. If you can relate prayers, and your whole teaching for that matter, to their egos you have hope of reaching them. If not, put in an

**HELP!**

early application for a different grade for next year. There's a "something" some teachers have that can get through to the super-cool, but it's rare. If you don't have it, you have "something else" just right for another type of class. Most of all, try not to let yourself dislike students like this (this can be difficult); if they are spoiled rotten, it really isn't their fault. They will need God, someday, a lot more than they now know. Not remembering this can make you disgusted with both your class and yourself, and has led to too many potentially good teachers giving up before they ever really got started.

A final problem is the prayer experiment (and there will be some) that bombs completely. Not even the most put-together teacher is disaster free, and we might as well realistically accept this fact. A failure may be the teacher's fault, through lack of preparation or choosing the wrong thing for the wrong time, but it's just as likely to be the fault of the class. We can even blame our flops on crossed stars or conjunctive planets if it will help us laugh them off, which we must do. There's bound to be that terrible moment when, halfway through some experiment, you realize that you're alone. And no alone is *more* alone than the teacher who has lost his class, with 40 minutes still to go! Often, a little extra enthusiasm in your voice and manner will hook those students who haven't yet completely left you, mentally. The worst tone you can take is that of the martyr-teacher (even a more obnoxious character than the martyr-mother), whose lumpy throat and sagging face say, "After all the time I spent preparing this class, how can you not appreciate me?" Off with her head.

If something you've started is really unbearable, cut it short and admit that it's rotten. Not taking our experiments and our failures too seriously (no matter how seriously we take prayer) is a good precedent for our students and reinforces for them the experimental nature of "lab work" in prayer. We should feel free to say "What a mess that was" occasionally and know all will learn from the experience.

Failures from time to time will only ruffle our fur if we feel all depends on us, and forget to make room in our minds for dependence on both God and our students—in other words, if we have fat heads!

## EVALUATING CLASSROOM PRAYER

Evaluating spiritual growth is enormously hard, almost impossible. God alone knows for sure who is coming closer to him, and how he gets there. We can try to get a little insight from our students, however, as they attempt to evaluate their progress in prayer. Half or two-thirds of the way through the year we can discuss this, or have another anonymous questionnaire on what's happening ("Yes, Mark, you can disguise your handwriting"). The choice depends mainly on how open your students are, and on their age. Questions could be along these lines:

- Of all the types of prayers we've tried, which do you like best? Can you explain why?

- Which do you like least?  Can you explain why?

- Which don't work at all for you right now?

- Using the usual school grades (A, B, C, D, F), can you give a general grade to the prayer experiments we've had, based on whether or not you feel they've helped you draw closer to God? (This isn't easy.)

- Would you suggest that I have prayer experiments for my class next year?

Answers to the last question should be taken with a grain of salt, because a student's immediate reaction will probably be, "We had to do it; why should those kids get out of it?"  While a questionnaire like this isn't completely conclusive, still it tells us something about growth and reinforces the students' awareness of how seriously you, the teacher, take this whole matter of prayer. Done midway through the year, it provides some guidelines for future choices of experiments. Do more of what works best.

Best of all, an occasional student may send you on the sort of trip only teachers take with a remark like: "I feel turned on to God for the first time in my life" or "I thought at first that you really had flipped out, but now I'm not so sure. . . ."

Something's happening!

# chapter 3
# SIMPLE
# PRAYERS

We turn now to specific types of prayers and the prayer experiments. By "simple prayers" we mean the sort religion teachers have always used — prayers everyone knows by heart, prayers we read from others' books, and made-up-on-the-spot prayers. All are useful, valid prayers and sometimes they are the very best possible, even the only possible, kind.

However, since these simple prayers have been the mainstays of most religion students since their babyhood, by the time these same students come to us all they know are rote prayers, prayers you say instead of prayers you pray (to use Thomas Merton's distinction).

We can use the prayer experiments in this chapter for variety in between our "fancy" experiments, and for days when simplicity seems particularly needed.

When reading from books of prayers written by someone else, there are a couple of important points to hang on to. The first is that any prayer book we choose should be written in "real" language, the language of today rather than that of Queen Victoria's times. We may have cut our teeth on prayers like

"O God, Thou who knowest every breath I take, lead Thou me toward Thy eternal beatific dwelling . . ."

Our students will take wing mentally (maybe physically too) if we use language like that with them. They will probably respond, however, to the same thought worded

"Lord, you're right with me all the time. Help me make it to heaven . . ."
Bury all your elegant prayer books, at least as far as classroom use goes, and stock up on some like the Rev. Malcolm Boyd's *Are You Running With Me, Jesus?* (New York: Avon Books, 1967. 75 cents), probably the best-known "mod prayer book."

Secondly, our students must be aware that reading a prayer doesn't necessarily equal praying. If we go back to the definition of prayer in Chapter 1, where prayer is equated with contacting God, we're reminded that an intellectual activity like reading isn't enough by itself to make contact. The will must be involved too. Therefore, any time someone reads a prayer for the class, it's a good idea for the teacher to remind all that they must bridge the gap between reading and praying by trying to make the writer's words truly their own.

Spontaneous spur-of-the-moment praying is perhaps the best kind of prayer there is, as Experiment No. 9 suggests. Many of the more elaborate prayer experiments in this book also feature off-the-cuff prayers, and the teacher may often, perhaps always, find that he is the only member of the class willing to open his mouth for this sort of prayer. In fact, he may have to make up these prayers for the entire year if no one responds to his invitations.

This can be discouraging, but really shouldn't be surprising. How many of us, at our students' age, would have freely tried to speak to God in front of a whole group of kids? The surprising thing is to find that there are individual boys and girls, and sometimes even whole classes, who rise above the fear of looking "too holy" and offer to pray out loud. If you don't have any such breakthroughs, keep smiling and keep praying, for your own example of easiness with the Lord can have a tremendous effect you never see.

# Memorized Prayers

# Tearing Up the "Our Father"

## EXPERIMENT NUMBER

**BACKGROUND:** In this first experiment we attempt to break down the universal bad habit of rattling off prayers by memory. Teachers will want to research and/or think through the meaning of the Lord's Prayer before class.

**MATERIALS:** None.

**CURRICULUM TIE-IN:** God the Father; prayer; atheism; communication, the bible, Jesus.

**PREPARATION OF CLASS:** Usual (cf. explanation pages 21-22)

---

"How many times in your life would you guess you have said the Lord's Prayer, the 'Our Father'? . . .

*(Note answers on board.)*

"Now, would you like to estimate the percentage of these times you really gave serious thought to the words of this prayer? . . .

*(as above)*

"Is there a difference between saying a prayer and praying? . . .

*(Explore as time permits.)*

"There's an old saying, 'familiarity breeds contempt.' What does it mean? . . .

"That's right. Often when we get to know something very well, we get so used to it that we completely forget to prize it—and this can happen with people too. What examples can you think of from your own experience? . . .

*(Taking parents and family for granted; roofs over heads; meals on tables; school and church, etc.)*

"Well, the same thing can happen with prayers. When you were little, you learned the 'Our Father,' and you learned where this prayer came from. Where *did* it come from? . . .

*(Jesus gave it to his apostles as a model for prayer. See Mt 6 and Lk 11.)*

"There's probably not a Christian alive who hasn't said this beautiful prayer so often that he or she hasn't taken it for granted, said it without thinking. Today we're going to try to do something about that for ourselves.

*(Include yourself in this category; have you a story of how you sometimes sit through church like a zombie, never giving thought to what you say?)*

"Who will volunteer to come up in front of the class and pretend to be a boy or girl raised as an atheist? . . . and, by the way, what's an atheist? . . .

*(Try to pick someone who doesn't say much in class, but let it be voluntary.)*

"Here's ......................., who has been raised without any belief in God. Now, let's try to explain the Lord's Prayer to him, phrase by phrase, so that he will have an understanding of what we mean when we pray it. . . .

"Who'll begin? Explain to ...................., please, what we mean when we say 'Our Father, who art in heaven.' . . .

*(Go through the prayer, a phrase or thought at a time, letting different students explain it and the "atheist" challenge them whenever he can. Pay special attention to understanding of "hallowed" (holy), the kingdom coming "on earth," "daily bread" (more than just food), and the implications of the forgiveness phrase.)*

33

"......................., do you think you understand this Christian prayer? . . . Is there anything else you'd like to ask about it? . . .

(Your "atheist" may side-track into proofs against the existence of God or other matters not directly connected with the prayer; these can be saved until the experiment is finished so that your main purpose — which is to pray—doesn't get lost.)

"Now we've torn the Lord's Prayer apart, and I wonder if you'd help me put it back together. Let's pray it together, slowly, each trying his best to concentrate on the meaning of each word and thought. Will you pray it with me? . . . 'Our Father,' etc. . . .

(Recite prayer slowly, or you might ask if anyone wants to lead the class; whenever a student offers to pray, be sure to thank him sincerely.)

"Good. Let's keep this experiment in mind the next time we say the Lord's Prayer in church or with a group. It's pretty special, isn't it? . . ."

(If time allows, this could lead naturally to a discussion of Jesus and prayer, as mentioned in Chapter 2; even if you have touched on this before, the thoughts bear reviewing.)

**DATE TRIED:**                    **TIME:**                    **REPEAT?:**


**RESULTS:**

# The "My Father"

## EXPERIMENT NUMBER 2

**BACKGROUND:** This simple experiment can be done any time after Experiment No. 1. Again, it's a closer look at the prayer of prayers, an attempt to appreciate it with fresh eyes and ears.

**MATERIALS:** None.

**CURRICULUM TIE-IN:** God the Father; prayer; especially petition.

**PREPARATION OF CLASS:** Usual.

| | |
|---|---|
| "The books say there are four things people pray about, four themes of prayer. Do you know what these are? . . . | *(List on board: praise of God, thanksgiving, sorrow for offending God, petition, or asking for things we need.)* |
| "Which of these four types of prayer do you think you use the most? . . . which next? . . . next? . . . least? . . . | *(Vote, and write decisions on board next to list.)* |
| "We talked about the 'Our Father' in an earlier prayer experiment. Which of the four types of prayer do you think it is? . . . | *(not only petition, but also praise of God and sorrow)* |
| "There are three themes in the 'Our Father.' These, plus the fact that Jesus gave us this prayer, make it very special. You'll notice also that the Lord's Prayer is in the plural. . . . What do I mean? . . . | *("our Father," "give us," "our daily bread")* |

"Good. And this fact—that we pray in the plural, for all of us—makes the Lord's Prayer especially useful for church services and group prayer.

"Let's do something with this famous prayer now to change it a little. Let's make it a little more personal by changing it from the plural to the singular. We'll change all the 'ours' to . . . ? . . . and each 'us' to . . . ? . . . and the 'we' to . . . ? . . .

*(These and the following substitutions might be written on the board: my, me, I.)*

"And to make it even more our own, let's get rid of some of the old-fashioned words. What could take the place of 'art'? . . . and of 'hallowed'? . . . of 'thy'? . . .

*("is," "holy," "yours"; in the extended version, "thine" would become "yours.")*

"Now, with these changes, how would our prayer sound? Let's put it together once, as a group, and then take time to try to pray the 'My Father' to ourselves. See if it takes on any new sense for you.

"My Father, who is in heaven, holy be your name. Your kingdom come, your will be done on earth as it is in heaven. Give me this day my daily bread, and forgive me my trespasses as I forgive those who trespass against me. And lead me not into temptation, but deliver me from evil. . . .

*(once through with class, using board)*

*(if you're continuing, "for yours is the kingdom and the power and the glory, forever and ever. . .")*

36

"And we usually end with 'Amen.' How could that be translated into today's language? . . .

("so be it," or in the words of the Beatles' song, "let it be")

"Good. Now for those who would like to, let's take a few seconds to quietly pray the 'My Father,' as we've just run through it, to ourselves. See if you can really concentrate on the meaning of the words in relation to your life. . . .

(If you bow your head slightly and obviously try the experiment along with the class, most students will follow suit.)

"You might want to try this idea with other very familiar prayers you've said over and over all your life. What other ones would be good prayers to personalize? . . ."

**DATE TRIED:**                **TIME:**                **REPEAT?:**


**RESULTS:**

# A Psalm for Today

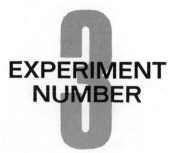

## EXPERIMENT NUMBER 3

**BACKGROUND:** This experiment logically builds on the experience of Experiment No. 2, although it could be used before No. 2. The idea of the bible in modern dress is as old as the early Christian artists who dressed Jesus and his contemporaries in the styles of their own eras (see, especially, Fra Angelico's or Giotto's famous frescoes of the life of Christ, with everyone dressed in late medieval Italian style)—and as new as each class of students who come to us. Paraphrasing scripture in modern terms is a widely used religious education method, of course, and has applications in art, dramatics, music and writing, as well as prayer.

**MATERIALS:** Bible; Psalm 23 ("The Lord Is My Shepherd") copied on half of board, with the other half left blank.

**CURRICULUM TIE-IN:** Psalms, Old Testament; God the Father; hope; faith; God in everyday things.

**PREPARATION OF CLASS:** Usual. Whatever background on the Psalms you want to add to the little in the experiment.

"Today we're going to take a look at the Psalms. You all know, I think, that the Psalms are . . .

*(the hymns of the Old Testament)*

"And many were written by a very famous king, King . . .

*(David)*

"Very good! Even though hundreds of years old, the Psalms seem to express the feelings of men of all times. They've always been popular. Where do you hear them used today? . . .

*(readings of the Mass; many folk hymns (Clap Your Hands by Ray Repp is Psalm 47 and Psalm 19, in part); Psalm 8 has been called the Moon Psalm, because it was quoted in connection with the Apollo flights.)*

"Jesus knew and quoted from the Psalms, as did all educated Jewish people of his time. Can you remember any times when he spoke words from the Psalms? . . .

*(on the cross, Ps 22: 2, see Mt 27: 46; on Palm Sunday, Ps 8: 3, see Mt 21: 16; at the Last Supper, Ps 69: 5, see Jn 15: 25)*

"Perhaps the most famous of all the Psalms is Psalm 23, 'The Lord Is My Shepherd.' I've written it here on the board, and I wonder if any of you have learned it by heart some time in the past. . . . This psalm is thought to have been written by King David, who was a shepherd at one time in his life. He used the example of God as a shepherd and the believer as a sheep, because that was what he knew and what his people knew. Do you know any shepherds? . . .

"We can understand what David meant, but it might be fun to try to write this psalm in the language of today, using comparisons that people are familiar with here in America. If you wanted to use the general outline of Psalm 23, but make it very meaningful to people who just couldn't grasp the idea of God being like a shepherd, what could you do? . . . What *could* God be like? . . .

*(If you have it available, you'll want to have someone read the paraphrase of Psalm 23 in God Is For Real, Man (New York, Association Press, 1966. $1.75), where tough kids from the streets wrote that the Lord was like their probation officer. See what your class comes up with, no matter how far out, avoiding—if possible—family comparisons; "The Lord is like my father" is an abominable thought to the boy or girl whose father is a bum. Some safer suggestions, if no one's imagination is clicking: The Lord can be like a navigator on a space flight, or like someone in the area known to all your students for his kindness, or —even—like a favorite teacher.)*

"Good! Now, let's go through the psalm, phrase by phrase, changing the ideas from those that fit sheep and shepherds, to those that fit our example of the Lord. . . .

*(Solicit ideas and rewrite the psalm verses, once the class o.k.'s them, on the blank half of the board opposite the original psalm.)*

"Here we have a psalm for today. Of course, the old version has a beauty that is timeless, but let's see how ours sounds when we put it together. Can we pray this together now, not just reading it from the board, but praying it and trying to make the words apply to our own lives? . . .

*(Sometimes group readings like this work better if the teacher is in back, not up front being boss.)*

"Very nice. I'll leave our version of Psalm 22 on the board so you can copy it after class if you'd like to save it."

**RESULTS:**

**REPEAT?:**

**DATE TRIED:**                    **TIME:**

# Prayer Readings

# God Speaks to Me

## EXPERIMENT NUMBER 4

**BACKGROUND:** This experiment is designed to increase familiarity with the bible, and help students feel it can be relevant to their lives. If the teacher feels uneasy about interpreting scripture in this off-the-cuff fashion, he can select a reading from the bible ahead of class. That, however, is "stiffer," and stiffness with scripture is what we would like to dispel.

**MATERIALS:** Bible. If each student has, or can bring in, a bible, so much the better. Can you get one of the new picture bibles?

**CURRICULUM TIE-IN:** Bible; revelation.

**PREPARATION OF CLASS:** Usual. Many classes also have bible shrines, set up by students and/or teacher, with candles, banners, flowers or plants, and other decorations around the bible.

---

"How do you feel about reading the bible—honestly? . . .

*(See if you can get past the what-does-teacher-want-me-to-say answers, better known as "Mickey Mouse answers.")*

"Many people say they are afraid to read, or even open a bible. Why do you think this is so? . . .

*(Bibles associated with church services, which seem superformal; most bibles don't look very readable — gold-rimmed pages, etc.; language of many is old-fashioned, etc.)*

"Today bibles are being printed with pictures of our times, and modern language, and in paperback instead of leather and gold. They're much more approachable, aren't they? . . .

(If you can dig up a very fancy old bible to compare with a modern version — the Alba House New Testament *is* good —this point is made very clearly.)

"Well, you know that when God gave us the bible he used a handful of men who lived in a small country a few thousand years ago to put his words down. But he meant it to be for all people at all times and in all places. . . . That means you, Jim, and Mary Ellen, and Debbie, and me, and everyone here in (your town) right now.

"And if God was writing for us, we should take the trouble to see what he said. Let's open the bible somewhere and see if we can understand how the verses we pick at random have anything to do with our lives. . . . Who would like to try this? . . .

(Let someone open bible at any point; read a few verses, starting and ending at a logical break in the text. The gospels are probably the easiest to understand, especially on the spur of the moment.)

"What do you think God is saying to us in this passage? . . . What do these words, written so long ago, have to do with us in the 1970's? . . .

(Yes, there is a chance—about one in a thousand—that you or a student can misinterpret the reading; run this slim risk to gain the end of this prayer experiment, familiarity with God's word. If the passage is too difficult, just say so and try another; explain that much of what is in the bible needs study to be interpreted well—but much of it doesn't.)

"Now, I'd like to ask someone to read these verses over again, this time as a prayer. . . Who'd like to do this? . . . Remember, one form of prayer is leaving ourselves open to God's voice—or his words, if you prefer. These words in the bible *are* his words; let's see now, as we listen, if we can let him make contact with us today. . . .

*(Volunteer reads, prayerfully rather than instructively.)*

"If you have a bible at home, you might want to try this experiment again. Some people do it every day of their lives. If you don't have a bible, you can try it before or after class with our classroom bible. And if the passage you open to is too difficult for you, try another. What do you think of this sort of praying (also known as the 'lucky dip' method)? . . . Which way is the 'action' going—from us to God, as usual, or from God to us? . . ."

*(Not a very subtle question, as you've loaded it, but an important distinction to make.)*

**DATE TRIED:**　　　　　　　　　**TIME:**　　　　　　　　　**REPEAT?:**

**RESULTS:**

# The Newspaper Prayer

## EXPERIMENT NUMBER 5

**BACKGROUND:** This experiment is one of many designed to remind students of how God is active in daily events, and of how we are surrounded by reminders of him.

**MATERIALS:** A separate newspaper or section of a newspaper for each student. Lacking this, a variety of newspaper clippings could be substituted.

**CURRICULUM TIE-IN:** God in everyday things; people; communication; revelation.

**PREPARATION OF CLASS:** Usual. Give out papers.

---

"Today, for our prayer experiment, everyone has a newspaper. Each is full of stories about people, some sad, some happy. These are all God's people, whether they're in the world news or the obituary column or on the sports page. . . .

"We're going to do three things with our papers. First, would you please look through them and choose some item that interests you? It can come from any section; it can be a story or an ad or a cartoon or a picture. . . .

*(If you have many sports enthusiasts, ask that only three or four choose something from the sports pages, otherwise you'll have a prayer experiment top-heavy with shutouts or touchdowns.)*

"Now, second, try to decide what connection the item you've chosen has with God. Is that very hard? Who can give us an example? . . .

*(War stories are connected with why God allows evil—but save the discussion on that for after the prayer experiment; a grand slam home run story leads to the idea of man using his God-given talents, etc.)*

45

"Who's stuck? Some things are easier to relate to God than others, but all have some sort of connection. Let's see if we can help anyone. . . .

(Go around class asking if each has made the connection of his article to God; those who haven't, discuss their item with the class.)

"Finally, the prayer step of this experiment is this: If each of the items from the papers has something to do with God, we can find material in it for a prayer. For instance, an engagement announcement might lead to a prayer for the couple to be married, or for all about to be married, or about marriage in general, or even about the marriage you may someday be part of yourself. . . .

"Let's be still for about a minute. First, think, then pray. . . .

(Allow a minute or so.)

"I wonder if anyone would be willing to share his prayer with the rest of us, or maybe just the ideas which were in his prayer. . . .

"Newspapers are good reminders of God's presence in our world today. What are some other reminders we have—non-religious reminders, that is? . . ."

(TV, magazines, billboards, movie displays and marquees, songs, radio, etc.)

**DATE TRIED:**                **TIME:**                **REPEAT?:**

**RESULTS:**

# The Historical Prayer Book

## EXPERIMENT NUMBER 6

**BACKGROUND:** Your students have probably been making scrapbooks since kindergarten; it's still a good idea, although you will want to soft-sell it, rather than insist that anyone contribute.

**MATERIALS:** A scrapbook or loose-leaf notebook. Pencils and paper.

**CURRICULUM TIE-IN:** Prayer; witness; the future.

**PREPARATION OF CLASS:** Usual. Previous assignment: Bring in a prayer you have written and *not* signed which in some way reflects the decade in which we are living right now. The prayer can be on any subject, but should be made contemporary by references to current events, names, music, books, fads and/or by using the language of today.

---

"Has anyone ever read old letters from the past? Did you raid your mother's old love letters? . . . or grandma's? . . . Or did you ever discover an old diary? . . .

*(Ask for a few examples.)*

"They're interesting, aren't they? Old prayer books are interesting too; they seem very out of date. I'm sure you've all brought in your assignment, a contemporary prayer. If for some strange reason you don't have yours with you—the dog ate it? Your little sister hid it?—you can take time to do the assignment now while we're getting ready for the prayer experiment. . . .

*(Dogs eat the strangest things; have pencil and paper ready for those with hungry canine pets.)*

"What we're going to do is put together a prayer book for the people of the year 20..... We'll put the prayers you have written (or are writing) in it, and if anyone likes he can add art work or articles on religion today. We can take a picture of this class and our building, and put that in the book with our names.

*(Choose date one hundred years hence.)*

*(If you suggest this, follow through.)*

47

"Before we take a look at the prayers you've written, let's see if we can decide how to preserve this book of ours for the people of one hundred years from now. . . .

(The pastor can be asked to put the book with the church records; some local history buff may be collecting examples of today's culture in your town—newspaper feature editors usually know the names of such people; the library or local historical society might accept it; a new building may be planned with a "time capsule cornerstone"—local contractors might know.)

"Who would like to investigate some of these ideas and report back to us? . . .

"Today we'll 'try on' a few of those prayers you've written, to see how they feel. Now that you know what's going to be done with your prayers, you can sign them if you like. Will you please pass them up? . . . I'll pick a few at random and ask someone to read them for us. . . .

(Collect, pick out a few that look pretty good at first glance.)

"Who'd like to read this one? . . . This will be our prayer experiment for today, and so I'd like to remind you that in order for each of us to pray, we have to do more than just listen to .............. read. What do we have to do? . . .

(Try to make the words of the prayer our own, if possible; it's not always possible, and that's all right too.)

"Let's try one more. Who'll read this one? . . . See if you can make this prayer your prayer as .................. reads it. . . .

"Is there anyone who'd like to put these prayers in our scrapbook? . . . Anyone who's good at lettering and would like to make a title page and a dedication? . . . What should these say? . . .

"And remember, if you see any good pictures which fit the prayers, or can draw any, or want to write something else for this prayer book, just add to it before or after class. It will, some-day, give the people who come after us a good idea of how we felt about our faith now in 19.... . . . We'll hear from .................. as soon as possible about ideas for saving this for your great-great-grandchildren."

*(You now have a supply of prayers for use in other classes; quickie prayer experiments can be created by reading— and praying—one or two of these prayers from the book. Try to use all that show any decent ef-fort at some time in the year.)*

*(Collect any pencils you gave out.)*

**DATE TRIED:**                    **TIME:**                    **REPEAT?:**

**RESULTS:**

# A Prayer That Wasn't Meant to Be

**EXPERIMENT NUMBER 7**

**MATERIALS:** Extra examples of "prayers that weren't meant to be" (see preparation of class) in case students don't come up with much.

**CURRICULUM TIE-IN:** God in everyday things; communication, revelation.

**PREPARATION OF CLASS:** Usual. Previous assignment: Look for and copy some piece of writing (from a novel, a speech, a poem, the lyrics of a song, a TV show, etc.) which *could* be a prayer, although it wasn't meant to be. For example, from one of the popular Hardy Boys' mysteries comes this line:

> "We've already stretched our luck, but if we take it slow, we should make it." (*Footprints Under the Window,* Franklin W. Dixon, New York, Grosset and Dunlap, 1965.)

and a French grammar might offer:

> "I love you. I have loved you. I will love you."

"Now you all have done your assignment, of course, and I hope your dogs and baby sisters haven't gotten into your papers. Who thinks they found a pretty good prayer somewhere that wasn't meant to be a prayer? . . .

*(Surely someone will have brought something.)*

"................, if you'd read what you found to the class, we'll use that for our prayer today. Once again, what are the ground rules for distinguishing between praying and listening to someone read a prayer? . . .

*(See, as reader reads, if you can make the speaker's words the words of your own heart.)*

"How many felt that ......................'s prayer worked for them? . . . Who has another 'prayer that wasn't meant to be'? . . .

*(If everyone brought something in, a remarkable possibility, collect and save for future classes.)*

"I found a couple of good 'nonprayers,' too; at least, they worked for me. Will you pray them with me? . . .

"The first is from the first act of *Hamlet,* and the words are spoken by a young gentleman to a ghost:

> Speak to me;
> If there be any good thing to be done,
> That may to thee do ease and grace to me,
> Speak to me . . . .

*(You might have asked, previously, what your students were reading in English, or what they read the preceding year, and go to those novels, plays and poems for your examples.)*

"And in *Treasure Island*—how many have read it?— . . . Captain Smollet has some words about outfitting his ship, which could also be a prayer from someone whose life needs help. If that's the case with you, see if this works as a prayer. . . .

> . . . you've heard me very patiently, saying things that I could not prove, hear me a few words more. . . . I see things going, as I think, not quite right. . . .

"You might keep on the lookout for more of these 'prayers that weren't meant to be,' and bring them in throughout the year. Watch new ad slogans and commercials especially. These reminders of God are all around us, and are one of his ways of speaking to us today."

---

**DATE TRIED:**                **TIME:**                **REPEAT?:**


**RESULTS:**

# Letter from a Friend

## EXPERIMENT NUMBER 8

**BACKGROUND:** This experiment is based on the "If Jesus came today" theme, also used in dramatics, art, music and other media.

**MATERIALS:** One pencil and piece of paper. You may want to refer to a bible.

**CURRICULUM TIE-IN:** Brotherhood, community; communication; New Testament, epistles; Jesus; early Church history.

**PREPARATION OF CLASS:** Usual.

---

"Let's start this prayer experiment with a little bible review. You know that after Jesus died he ................... . . . and then, the gospels tell us that he stayed on earth ................... days . . . and then ................... . . . What plans did he make before he left to keep his work alive? . . .

*(rose)*
*(40)*
*(ascended to heaven)*
*(Pentecost and the Holy Spirit would bring strength to his followers, who would lead the Church and spread Christianity.)*

"Very good! And, of course, there was a lot of work for these men to do, wasn't there? The known world, even in those days, was pretty large for the small band of Jesus' followers to take care of. In the New Testament we find several epistles; what's an epistle? . . . and would you guess how many epistles are in the New Testament? . . . and do you remember who wrote them? . . .

*(a letter)*
*(21)*
*(Sts. Paul, James, Peter, John and Jude)*

"Fine! Now, these epistles, or letters, were written to people in various cities or provinces of the Roman Empire. Who knows why they were written? . . . and what were some of the places in which these new Christians lived? . . .

*(to encourage the Christian converts in these places to persevere in their faith)*

*(Corinth, Galatia, Ephesus, Philippi, etc.)*

52

"The apostles who wrote the epistles couldn't be with their converts and fellow Christians as much as they wanted to be, and so they wrote to them and sent reminders of their teaching, and prayed for them in their letters.

"Today I'm going to ask you to do some imagining for our prayer experiment. Could you imagine that instead of Jesus living, dying, rising and ascending in Palestine, almost two thousand years ago, he had waited until our time? Suppose he had been born in America, say, about 1935 or so, and Christianity had begun here, about the time you were in grade school. . . .

"If the facts of the story were repeated, about this time his chief followers, or apostles, would be spreading around America and around the world, teaching about Jesus and baptizing new Christians. They would be even less able than the first apostles to keep up with their flocks, and they would have to write letters to different cities, just as the first apostles did.

"Do you begin to see where we're heading? . . . Good! Now who'd like to be the apostle to this little band of Christians here in ....................? . . . We'll help you write your letter.

*(your city or town)*

*(Give paper and pencil to apostle, who can come to the front and put together a letter from the class' ideas.)*

"This will just be a short letter, Apostle ............. First, what should the apostle say to the people of ................? . . . and what should come next? . . .

*(probably some sort of greetings)*

*(perhaps a question or two on how his converts are doing)*

53

"Let's have the apostle ask for prayers for the different needs of ................. Apostle ................, how would you want to start that part of your letter? . . .

(something along the lines of "I hope you will pray, as I do, for the following needs of the city of ....................")

"Well, what are the needs of our city? . . .

(List them; give apostle time to write them down.)

"And, finally, how do you think he should end his letter? . . .

(If ideas are slow in coming, you might see what Peter and Paul did before you.)

"That's fine. Now Apostle ................, you're going to give this letter to a messenger; who's the messenger? . . .

(If you get more than one volunteer, try to pick the better or best reader.)

"And, messenger, you're going to bring the letter from the apostle to this little group of new Christians here in ....................— that's the rest of us. And you're going to read us the letter from our friend and teacher. And, we, when you reach the part about praying for the needs of our city, will try to make that our prayer too. . . . Is everyone ready? . . .

(Messenger reads, and if you set example of prayerful listening, class should follow along.)

"What we've done, in sort of a roundabout way, is pray for the needs of our city, as well as for ourselves. What do you think any of us could do to help out with some of these needs? . . ."

**DATE TRIED:**                **TIME:**                **REPEAT?:**

**RESULTS:**

# Spontaneous Prayers

# The Best Prayer of All

**EXPERIMENT NUMBER**

**BACKGROUND:** This experiment aims at creating a familiarity with spontaneous prayer had by all too few students. It's the most important sort of praying we can do, for it is the basis for an adult relationship with God. If you do this all the time with your classes, you already believe this; if you don't, see if this helps you get started.

**MATERIALS:** None.

**CURRICULUM TIE-IN:** Anything and everything.

**PREPARATION OF CLASS:** Usual.

"Today, rather than having an elaborate prayer time, why don't we just make up a simple prayer? Is there anyone who would like to do this for us? . . .

*(Avoid a down-in-the-chops look if no one offers; keep the mood on the upbeat. If you do have a taker, accept his prayer gladly and praise him sincerely for it.)*

(If you have to do it yourself) "Well, I'll make up a prayer for us then. Help me out by giving me a few suggestions as to what would be a good *topic* to pray *about*. . . .

*(Again, be very encouraging and accepting of any ideas.)*

(If no suggestions are forthcoming) "How about a prayer for Bob's mother, who is sick, and for everyone else we know who's ill. . . .

*(or for people we know who are unhappy; or about some local or national or world event; or in thanksgiving for particular blessings in our lives; or for a good vacation or holiday)*

56

"Take a few seconds to think of whom you know who should be included in this prayer. . . .

"Lord, one of us has a parent who isn't well, and all of us know
others who need their health. We ask your help for them,
and for all who are sick. Amen."

*(Keep it simple and make
it up as you go along; if
your spontaneous prayers
don't sound spontane-
ous, none of the kids
will ever offer for fear of
not being able to match
your "professional" pray-
ing.)*

"Now, that's all there is to making up a prayer. I'm sure you all do
that on your own, and maybe some other time someone in the
class will do it for all of us. Once you get started, it's easy . . .
or don't you think so? . . ."

**DATE TRIED:**                    **TIME:**                    **REPEAT?:**

**RESULTS:**

# A Collection Prayer

**EXPERIMENT NUMBER 10**

**BACKGROUND:** The Collect is another basic sort of prayer, included here as an example for those who have never tried it. Save this experiment until the class has some easiness with prayer, in hopes they will feel free to speak out.

**MATERIALS:** None.

**CURRICULUM TIE-IN:** Anything and everything.

**PREPARATION OF CLASS:** Usual, plus a few thoughts on why students should contribute to prayer in the classroom. Each has what no one else can give to the group; by not contributing, he may be depriving everyone else of some insight of great value.

---

"Church services in many faiths often have a prayer called the Collect. Why would a prayer be called that? . . .

*(Write word on the board, pronounce it with accent on the first syllable.)*

"You see that it's the same as the word "collect," just pronounced differently. The idea is that the prayers of all the people are "collected" and offered to God. Today we're going to see if we can make up a Collect of our own prayers.

"First, we need a theme, an intention. Ideas? . . .

*(Accept gratefully any workable idea; those which just won't work, build on but don't reject out of hand.)*

(If no ideas) "How about a thanksgiving prayer? I'll start it off, and then if you're willing, see if you can each add the name of one thing for which you're thankful. Will you try it with me? . . .

"Dear God, we have so much to be thankful for, and we want you to know that we appreciate this. Thank you for . . .

*(Don't be afraid of a little silence; if it gets sticky, you can add to the prayer and then wait again. Even if no one breathes a word, don't register displeasure or disappointment outwardly; a short discussion— should this happen—on why people hesitate to pray even to this small extent could follow the experiment.)*

"Sometime you might take part in a worship service where there is only a small group of people—a home Mass or a prayer meeting. Much more of this 'shared prayer' is being done in such small groups, and this experiment gives you an idea of how it works."

**DATE TRIED:**             **TIME:**                      **REPEAT?:**

**RESULTS:**

# Do-It-Yourself Prayer

## EXPERIMENT NUMBER 11

**BACKGROUND:** Save this experiment for days when prayer hasn't been going so well; most students enjoy it a great deal, and it can be repeated with infinite variations. The theme is the same as that of Nos. 5 and 7, God present in all sorts of reminders around us, and thus reinforces them.

**MATERIALS:** Three or four objects, the more unusual the better, which you have related in some way (see below).

**CURRICULUM TIE-IN:** God in everyday things; symbols and signs.

**PREPARATION OF CLASS:** Usual.

---

"I've brought four things to class with me, and they're the basis for a prayer for today. I wonder if anyone can guess what I had in mind. . . .

*(Someone may come up with a connection completely different from yours; accept it graciously and toss yours out.)*

(If no one guesses) "Here's:

1) a bottle of glue (or paste)
2) a creepy crawler (or plastic Frankenstein or other repulsive thing)
3) a picture of a pig (or skunk, or rat)
4) a small plant

"What sort of prayer could be made out of these four items? . . .

*(This is just one of many possible ideas.)*

60

"How about this: 'O God, please stick to me (glue) even when I act like a monster or a pig, and please help me to keep growing every day (plant). . . .'

(Pause and allow time for each item to sink in amid groans.)

"Now we've pieced together the prayer, which isn't really the same as praying it. Would anyone like to *pray* the same prayer for all of us? . . . Let's pull ourselves together so it'll be a good prayer. Ready? . . .

(If no one has offered, you can repeat the prayer, this time prayerfully.)

"Reminders of God are all around us, and they work for us as reminders if we can remember to keep our eyes open. Why don't you each see if you can find a few things that go together to make up a prayer like this one? . . . See if you can stump us as to what connection they have to God and to us and to praying. . . ."

(and if anyone does bring in a do-it-yourself prayer, let him run the experiment.)

Another do-it-yourself prayer:

1) a can opener—'O Lord, help us to open our eyes . . .'
2) some goodies or cooking ingredients—'. . . so we can see all the good ingredients in ourselves and others . . .'
3) board eraser—'We'd like to wipe out all the things that . . .'
4) shoe— '. . . keep us from climbing closer to you.'

**DATE TRIED:**            **TIME:**            **REPEAT?:**

**RESULTS:**

## chapter 4
# PRAYERS WITH OTHER PEOPLE

Scripture seems to have been rewritten to read "wherever two or three are gathered together in my name . . . they will break up into small groups." Hardly a meeting occurs today where one isn't asked to turn to his neighbor(s) and share ideas, reactions, or at least the time of day.

This is fine, and equally fine in the classroom, as long as something is accomplished by the sharing. We must beware of overdoing a good thing, however, and we can also try to vary our types of groupings.

The simplest breakdown is into pairs (or dyads). Rather than have each student choose a partner, which can cause commotion and also hurt feelings, take a few seconds to pair off your boys and girls by saying "you and you" and "you and you," and so on. An odd student can be the teacher's partner. Depending on the subject to be shared, the giggle-quotient of the class, and the age of the students, you will have to decide if pairings of the same or the opposite sex work best. For eighth grade and under, pairs of the same sex are usually a happier choice.

Groups of three and four have a less personal tone than one-to-one pairings; here too it is helpful to divide a class yourself rather than let three or four sitting near each other automatically form a group. This is most easily done by putting a seating plan on the board for a particular class, with your divisions indicated. This way you can arrange to have a good leader in each group, along with a few followers.

If you use the small group technique often, whether for praying or for the body of a class, you will want to brief your students early in the year on some basic rules for good group functioning. Primary among these are:

- Everyone should try to contribute.

- Everyone *must* respect the opinions of others in the group. Negative remarks like "what a dumb idea" or "you idiot" are not allowed.

- All should try to stick to the topic.

- No one should dominate a group—if only one student has any ideas, he should try to draw out the others.

Be sure to call time on group discussions before they peter out into rigor mortis.

A different type of prayer with other people in this chapter is one based on a guest "witness talk," or a testimonial to one's faith. Evangelists like Billy Graham use this method very effectively, and of course they have large numbers of committed people from whom to select their select their speakers—but who can witness to your class?

We should remember that our students expect clergymen and people in religious life to love God. They are more captivated, usually, to find that the guy next door loves him too. This doesn't rule *out* professional church people as guest speakers, but it does rule *in* a lot of very down-to-earth lay men and women, and boys and girls. The author's experience has been that the most successful guest speakers in religion classrooms have been very average citizens—someone's mother or father, an older brother or sister, the man who runs the corner bar and grille or the Little League coach.

Also important to remember, when thinking of guest speakers for religion classes, is that some boys you teach may be under the misapprehension that religion is for their sisters and mothers, "women's stuff." For them, the witnessing of another boy or a man they can admire is especially valuable.

If you suspect or know that someone has a real working faith, ask him if he will come to your class and give a two-to-five-minute, off-the-cuff talk on "Why I am a Christian (Jew, Moslem, etc.)" or "The Part Religion Plays in My Life" or the like. Suggest that the talk be built around some incident in the person's life, so that it becomes a story rather than an abstract lecture in theology. You may find many a wonderful person who will be willing to tell about

—how his faith helped him through some crisis in his life.

—a dilemma he faced and overcame by drawing on the teachings of his religion.

—some time when he felt especially close to God.

—a time when he was without God, and what made him turn back.

Few speakers will have dramatic stories to tell, which is fine because most students suspect before they are far into their teens that they probably *won't* lead dramatic lives. They are able to identify best with stories of what happened at school, at home, on the job and with "my boy (girl) friend."

If you offer to let members of the class give such talks, and someone is brave enough to take you up on it, you may discover the best witness of all. Try, also, asking at the end of the year for volunteers to come back next year to talk to the "little kids" who will be in your next class.

Although only three prayer experiments are given here, you will see that each can be varied in many ways by changing the topic suggested. Prayers with other people can give our young people the chance to be and to meet "other Christs."

# "Where Two or Three Are Gathered. . ."

## EXPERIMENT NUMBER 12

**MATERIALS:** None.

**CURRICULUM TIE-IN:** Brotherhood, community; communication; problems of daily life; Jesus.

**PREPARATION OF CLASS:** Usual. Pair off students.

---

"Jesus once said, 'Where two or three are gathered together in my name, there am I in their midst.' What does that mean? . . . Does it mean anything special in connection with our gathering here in this religion classroom? Are we gathered in Jesus' name? . . .

*(Mt 18:20)*

"Yes, we are, aren't we? . . . and today we're going to gather in twos—like St. Matthew says—in Jesus' name. When we do that we have his word for it that he is in our midst.

"Everyone has a partner. Will you take the next 30 seconds to think of some problem you have about which you would feel free to tell this partner? . . .

*(or, instead of a problem, each could think of someone they love, or some need in the world, or anything which would serve as a prayer intention.)*

"Now, let's call everyone on the left of each pair 'person A,' and everyone on the right of each pair 'person B.' Will each A turn to his partner and tell him his problem? . . .

*(Fifteen seconds is plenty.)*

65

"And now will all the B's please turn to the A's and tell them their problems? . . .

"Next, we're going to take about 30 seconds, and this time we'll keep perfectly quiet. We're gathered in twos in the name of Jesus, and *he is* in our midst, and we'll use this time to ask him to help our partner with whatever his problem is. . . . Can you do that, silently, to yourself? . . . (You don't have to, of course.) . . .

"One of the very best ways we can help anyone is to pray for them, especially if we've come together as Christians. We all know this. How often do we do it? . . ."

**DATE TRIED:**                   **TIME:**                  **REPEAT?:**

**RESULTS:**

# The Mother Earth Prayer

**EXPERIMENT NUMBER 13**

**MATERIALS:** A variety of objects from nature to supplement those you have asked students to bring in (see below). Keep these out of sight.

**CURRICULUM TIE-IN:** Creation; God in everyday things.

**PREPARATION OF CLASS:** Usual. Also, beforehand, ask class members to each *smuggle* in some small piece of nature: a rock, a flower, a shell, a feather, a sponge, a nut, a branch, a pine cone, a piece of fur, grass or weeds, a fruit or vegetable, a log or piece of bark, a nest, leaves, a cork, etc. (One restriction: it cannot be alive and kicking.) You will have several such things on hand, as not everyone will remember (understatement of the year).

---

"Everyone has with him today—and please keep it hidden—something from the world of nature. Is there anyone who forgot to bring something? . . .

*(Secretly distribute something from your collection to each person who forgot.)*

"We're going to try a prayer experiment today, using these things, and first I'd like to pair you off into twosomes. . . .

"Now, you have ten seconds to figure out which person in each pair is older. . . .

*(just to provide variety on who speaks first, rather than always dividing into A and B, or right and left)*

"Will the younger person in each pair now close his eyes. No peeking allowed. And, now, younger person, hold out your left hand. . . .

"And older person, place the object from nature which you have in the hand of your partner. Younger partner, no peeking. . . .

"Now, younger person, without looking feel the thing you've been given. Try to figure out what it is. You can smell it, even taste it, and then start guessing what it is. When your partner says you're right, you can open your eyes. . . .

(You may have to call time if some are hopelessly stumped.)

"Now, reverse roles, this time with the older partner closing his eyes and receiving the piece of nature. Guess until you get the right answer. No one brought anything alive, did they? . . .

"That was the easy part. This is harder. I'd like to ask you to close your eyes again. Hold on to the piece of nature your partner has given you, and try to visualize it in its natural home. If it's a fruit, hanging on a tree; if it's a feather, part of a bird, flying in the air. . . .

"Finally, keeping your eyes closed, can you see if your contact with this piece of nature, which is part of God's creation of course, suggests to you any sort of communication with the One who made it? . . . I'll give you a couple of examples to get you started, and this will be our prayer for today. If you have a shell, you might think of the beach, and then of how peaceful it is in the cool, wet sand where this shell came from. Your prayer might be something like 'Lord, I need your peace. Please send me some.' Or a feather might take you up in the air and lead you to a prayer about flying above problems, and so on. . . .

(This is a good time for the practice of silence, something most students are not very comfortable with; we should try to inject short periods of silence in our busy classes —and lives—whenever we can do it without being artificial.)

68

"And finally, the last part of the experiment, IF you want to and only if you want to, tell your partners *about* your prayer. Notice that I didn't say 'tell your partners your prayer,' as that was something between you and God—if you were able to say something to him. But you might tell your partners how or if your item from nature led to a prayer, where it took you physically—the ocean, a garden—and what the connection to God was. . . .

"Each older person, please tell your partner if he or she has your permission to share your thoughts with the rest of the class (not your prayer, but your thoughts). . . .

"And each younger person, please tell your partner if he or she has your permission to share *your* thoughts with all of us. . . .

"How many have permission from their partners? . . .

"Good. Let's go around to these people and see what it is their partners have given them permission to reveal. When I get to you, tell us what piece of nature you gave your partner, whether you are the younger or older in your pair, and what your partner's thoughts and connection to God were from his piece of nature. . . ."

*(Allow time.)*

*(Call on everyone who had his hand up; it's much less difficult to report what someone else told you about bridging the gap from natural to supernatural than it is to tell your own thoughts.)*

**DATE TRIED:**                    **TIME:**                    **REPEAT?:**

**RESULTS:**

# A Witness Talk

**EXPERIMENT NUMBER 14**

**MATERIALS:** A guest speaker (see Chapter 4). Know his background, so you can introduce him well. Also, ask him in advance if he can/will stay for the whole class, or must leave after speaking. If he has to leave early, you'll want to say good-bye and thank him rather than have him slip out the door.

**CURRICULUM TIE-IN:** Whatever topics your speaker may touch on; witness; people.

**PREPARATION OF CLASS:** Usual. At the preceding class you may want to tell students there'll be a guest, and ask for their very best behavior.

---

"With us today is ......................, who's kind enough to take time to come and share some of his experiences and thoughts on his faith with us.

*(Add whatever background on your speaker is necessary.)*

(Speaker)

*(Please don't tolerate any poor behavior in the class while a guest is speaking; most students are so grateful for a new face before them that they're very attentive.)*

"Thank you, ........................... Does anyone have any questions he'd like to ask? . . .

"As you know, having ........................ here to talk with us is part of a prayer experiment. Would you see if you can help me list on the board some things from ........................ 's talk that might be suitable prayer subjects? . . .

*(You may have to do some leading here, as many students are reluctant to speak up in front of a newcomer, especially an adult. Also, you won't want to settle for broad topics related to your speaker's talk, but will want to bring them down to your students' lives; for example, don't just put "grace" on the board, but "grace—does it come to all of us?" or "grace—how does it reach me?" etc.)*

"Finally, and this is the reason for all our prayer experiments, can we make up a prayer about one or more of these subjects we've listed here? . . .

*(As always, you must be ready to pick up the ball and run—or pray. Perhaps your guest will be willing to do this if none of the students are, but be sure to check in advance with him.)*

"Thank you, ........................, very much, etc., etc."

**DATE TRIED:**                    **TIME:**                    **REPEAT?:**

**RESULTS:**

# chapter 5
# PRAYERS WITH PENCIL AND PAPER

This group of prayer experiments, using the most basic of classroom supplies, is an easy group for the teacher to implement and an easy group for students to attempt. They are easy for students because all are non-committing, non-threatening; they allow the student's most personal thoughts to remain completely private and anonymous unless he chooses to share them.

The major problem with pencil and paper prayers is being able to get your hands on (and keep) pencils and paper! This sounds ridiculous, but any experienced teacher knows that pencils disappear as if they were set with diamonds—if the students don't get 'em the other teachers will. The same is true of supplies of paper, and teachers usually end up dragging both items around with them for safekeeping. (Religion teachers are often faced with the added, somewhat incongruous, problem of finding their bibles swiped by other teachers. "Who stole my bibles?" ringing down the hall of a church school strikes a jarring note in an otherwise supportive setting!)

It took the author nine months to learn how to pass out pencils and paper without disrupting a class; this is one of those tiny but significant details that separate the men from the boys. One easy way is to have both pencils and paper on a desk or windowsill before class, and a note on the chalkboard (if you have one) saying, "Please get pencil and one sheet of paper." As everyone comes in, the teacher can call attention to the board. A second simple technique for distributing pencils and/or paper is to hand the exact number needed per row to the student at the end of each row, asking the kids to pass them down. Don't forget to collect your pencils at the end of class.

Notebooks (if the class remembers to bring them) help with the paper problem, and some pencil and paper prayer experiments can be done in textbook margins or inside covers.

This category of experiments is a logical one for further experimentation by students themselves; an assignment might even be to make up another pencil and paper prayer experiment. Who knows what possible leads to prayer might already be scribbled in the margins of math books and on the backs of report card envelopes?

# 2001 A.D.

## EXPERIMENT NUMBER 15

**MATERIALS:** Pencils and paper for all (unlined paper better).

**CURRICULUM TIE-IN:** Saints, purpose of life; human potential; the future; vocation.

**PREPARATION OF CLASS:** Usual. Explain that this is a drawing experiment, not an art contest. Pass out materials.

---

"Draw a quick picture of yourself as you think you might look in the year 2001 A.D. You'll be about — years old. What sort of clothes will you be wearing? . . .

*(Expect and allow for comparison of art work, laughter, moans, etc.)*

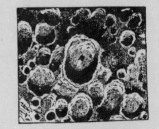

"Now, under your picture put your name . . . and your address as it might be in 2001. Would you choose this city? Or will you be, perhaps, across an ocean? Or on the moon? . . .

"Finally, *before* your name, put the letters 'S' and 'T' and a period, like this. . . .

*(Write "St." on board.)*

"What does it say? . . . that's right, 'saint,' 'Saint You.' . . .

*(Name some names in class: "St. Linda," "St. Debbie.")*

"Will you be a saint in 2001? . . .

*(more moans)*

"Well, if you won't be one by then, would you say that you'll be on your way to being one? . . . After all, one definition of a saint is 'someone who made it to heaven, or is on the way.'

*(If this is part of a lesson about sanctity, you can elaborate: Are we all called to be saints? Does it mean being a holy Joe? Never having any fun? Differentiate between "saint" and "Saint," the officially canonized variety.)*

"Let's take a minute to talk to God now, and we might ask him to help us get on the road to being 'St. .............................' by 2001 A.D. If you like, you could write your prayer under the picture. . . ."

*(Collect pencils.)*

**DATE TRIED:**                    **TIME:**                    **REPEAT?:**

**RESULTS:**

75

# Gifts Assortment Prayer

**EXPERIMENT NUMBER 10**

**MATERIALS:** Paper and pencils for all, the paper cut into various-sized rectangles to simulate packages or wrapped gifts. If you want to use colored paper or even real gift-wrapping paper, and perhaps colored pencils, so much the better.

If you have bulletin boards, clear one and have one pin or thumbtack in it for each student.

**CURRICULUM TIE-IN:** Gifts from God; thanksgiving.

**PREPARATION OF CLASS:** Give everyone one "gift package" and pencil.

"What do you think the piece of paper I've given you is supposed to be? . . .

"That's right; it's a picture of a gift, a present. You can make it look a little fancier if you want to add ribbons or some sort of decorations with your pencils. . . .

(masculine groans)

"Now, on this gift package, how about writing down one or more of the many gifts God has given you? Only put down things you wouldn't mind having read to the rest of the class. For instance, if you've been blessed with the world's most beautiful face you might not want us all to know you think that's the case. This would apply to all the girls in the class, of course. . . .

"When you're finished, will you please come up to the board a few at a time, and pin your 'gift package' to the bulletin board anyplace you like? . . .

*(If without a bulletin board, you can walk around with a piece of heavy poster paper and pins; the gifts can be stuck to that.)*

"Let's see what some of the gifts we have here are. . . .

*(Read all from bulletin board or have one of the students do it.)*

"Does all this suggest a prayer to anyone here? What do you usually say when someone gives you a gift? . . .

*(Be ready, as usual, to do it yourself should no one be brave enough to speak for the class.)*

"Thanks, ........................ That was just fine."

*(if someone offered)*

*(Collect pencils.)*

**DATE TRIED:**          **TIME:**          **REPEAT?:**

**RESULTS:**

# My Tombstone

## EXPERIMENT NUMBER 17

**MATERIALS:** Paper and pencils for all. Do you have any gravestone rubbings you can bring in?

**CURRICULUM TIE-IN:** Death; the future values, purpose of life; philosophy of life; faith, hope.

**VOCABULARY TO EXPLAIN:** epitaph.

**PREPARATION OF CLASS:** Pass out pencils and paper. The experiment lends itself to detailed dissection of students' attitudes toward death and dying, a most vital subject for religion classes.

---

"Today we're going to kill everyone off, or at least think about the fact that—someday—everyone's time will be up. Of course, I hope all of you will still be hanging around until the mid-2000's, but we just don't know, do we? . . .

*(As noted elsewhere, if any of your students has had a death in the immediate family, you will want to curb any flipness on this subject; what's suitable for the average student might be unbearable for the boy or girl who has lost a parent.)*

"On your paper, using the whole page, would you please draw a shape like this? . . .

*(On board, draw a tombstone shape.)*

"Who can guess what this is going to be? . . .

*(Avoid mentioning title of prayer experiment before this point.)*

78

"Now, at the top of this tombstone, would you put your name, and under your name the year you were born, then a hyphen, then four question marks. . . .

(On board, write your name in the tombstone; your birth year—or whatever you say is the year of your birth, a hyphen and ????)

"We're each designing a tombstone for ourselves. And the bottom half of the tombstone will have some thought that you would like people to remember you by, your epitaph.

"If you wander in old graveyards, you'll see lots of interesting verses or one-line thoughts, like 'He was a wonderful man' or 'She was never too busy to listen.' Maybe you'd like something like that. . . .

(Are there any interesting graveyards in your area you can recommend? You might try making rubbings of old tombstone carvings, many of which are fascinating. To a fairly smooth stone tape rice paper; rub charcoal or a dark pastel over the surface to bring out the raised stone carving on your paper. Ask permission of the cemetery caretaker before attempting this.)

"Or maybe you'd like to be remembered for your work. There's a dentist's grave in Scotland that has on the tombstone:
Stranger, tread this ground with gravity,
Dentist Brown is filling his last cavity.

"See if you can think of the right words for your tombstone. I'll give you a couple of minutes. . . .

(Allow for some mild outbursts and conversation while this is being done, as this is both a comic and deadly earnest exercise.)

"Those who finish first can add some grass. How about some flowers too? . . .

"Now, who'd like to read his epitaph to us? . . .

(Most students, if coaxed a little, will want to share their ideas.)

"Finally, I thought you'd enjoy hearing a couple of the famous comic epitaphs from old gravestones. Our ancestors were much more realistic about death than we are today. They knew it would come and made no bones about it—or about being prepared for it.

(No pun intended.)

"Here's a famous one from a tomb in Burlington, Vermont:
Here lies the body of our dear Anna,
Done to death by a banana;
It wasn't the fruit that dealt the blow,
But the skin of the thing that laid her low.

(These and many other interesting examples of resignation to death can be found in Comic Epitaphs (Mount Vernon, N.Y., Peter Pauper Press, 1957. $1.00), a good book for a religion classroom reference shelf.)

"And one found on a coal miner's grave reads:
Gone underground for good.

"A very sad, but down-to-earth, verse is on a baby's tombstone in
   Bennington, Vermont:
        Beneath this stone our baby lies,
        He neither cries nor hollers;
        He lived on earth just twenty days,
        And cost us forty dollars.

"How does that sort of attitude toward death differ from the way we
   feel today? . . .

"Finally, here's a famous old verse from a town named Medway:
        Beneath this stone, a lump of clay,
        Lies Uncle Peter Daniels;
        Too early in the month of May
        He took off his winter flannels.

*(Obviously, this part of
the prayer experiment
can be shortened or
omitted as you get to the
point, which is praying.)*

"Now, at last, does what we've done and what we've read suggest
   a prayer to anyone? . . .

*(Again, be ready with
some "quickie" of your
own if the need arises.)*

"Why not take your tombstone home and put it where you can look
   at it this coming week? . . ."

*(Collect pencils.)*

**DATE TRIED:**                    **TIME:**                    **REPEAT?:**


**RESULTS:**

# Happy Day Prayer

**EXPERIMENT NUMBER 18**

**MATERIALS:** Pencils and paper for all.

**CURRICULUM TIE-IN:** Thanksgiving, gifts from God; joy.

**PREPARATION OF CLASS:** Usual. Pass out paper and pencils.

"The prayer experiment we're going to do today is all done on paper. First, I'd like to ask you to divide your paper up into sections; this will remind you of first grade. Across the top, would you please fold or draw a top margin of about two inches? . . .

"Next, will you divide the space that's left into four equal rectangles, again either by folding or drawing lines? . . .

"Very good! Now, the reasoning behind this prayer experiment is as follows: All too often we get so busy griping and complaining about what's wrong in our lives, such as. . . .

*(Collect a few ideas on this point from the kids, who'll be all too happy to tell you of how mistreated they are by parents, siblings and—especially—teachers!)*

"Poor things! Well, anyway, we can spend so much time feeling sorry for ourselves, for all the reasons you've mentioned, that we forget how many things are right and good in our lives. Today we're going to stop, and think about the good things, even write them down. Best of all, we're going to take the time to thank God for all these good things, something many of us often fail to do.

(Surely you can think, here, of some appropriate example in your own life; did you spend yesterday grousing about this and that, while surrounded by all sorts of beautiful blessings? Who doesn't?)

"At the top of your paper, in the two-inch margin, would you write this, or something like it if you prefer to use your own words: 'Thanks, God, for the good things of ........................, 19 ....'?.

*(Use yesterday's date, or if you have evening classes, today's date.)*

"O.K. Now at the top of the first box on your paper please put this title: *GOOD THINGS I DID.* Under the title, can you list all the actions you took or activities you were part of yesterday —things like eating, sleeping, TV-watching—that you enjoyed? Try to think in terms of action words, verbs ending in '-ing.' . . .

*(Allow a couple of minutes; make your own list while students do theirs — you're not just Big Brother, but also a learner in the class.)*

"Good. Who'd like to share his list, or any part of his list with us? . . . The rest of us can add to our own lists as we hear good ideas from other people. . . .

*(This step can be omitted if you're pressed for time.)*

"Now, in the second box, please put this title: *GOOD PEOPLE I WAS WITH.* List as many people you can remember speaking to or just being with yesterday, who are good people to be with. Each time we are with someone who's good to be with, it rubs off a little on us. . . .

83

"At the top of the third box, the title will be: *GOOD EXPERIENCES.* This is a little different from what you listed in box one. By good experiences, we mean good things that happened to us, rather than things we actually did. For instance, did you get some interesting mail? Or did you spend time with your radio or record player on, letting the music wash over you?— that sort of thing. This is a little harder, isn't it? . . . See how many good experiences you can recall from yesterday, and list them in box three . . .

"And finally, box four will have the title *GOOD REMINDERS OF YOU.* Who's 'You'? . . . Right, it's God himself, and—as you know— he's filled his world with many reminders of himself. It's up to us to see them, and use them, and be reminded. What are a few examples of good reminders of God? . . .

*(The usual things mentioned are items from nature and religious objects in home, church or school; can you suggest a few less common reminders?: clocks—symbolic of our time here on earth, streets—symbols of the "road of life," and circles — found everywhere and symbolic of eternity.)*

"How many reminders of God that appeared in your life yesterday can you list in box four? . . .

*(If there's time, sharing whatever students were willing to share from this box would be interesting.)*

"Good. Now, tell me something. Have we *prayed* by writing 'Thanks, God. . . .' and by listing all sorts of good things from him? . . .

*(Several students may feel they have been in touch with God as they've written and thought; this is prayer. However, you will want to point out for those who have just done this as an exercise to this point, that writing words to God is not—necessarily—the same thing as praying.)*

"Let's take a half a minute or so now, to make sure that this is really a prayer experiment, not just a thinking experiment. Let's quietly read over everything we've written, this time *really* thanking God for the good things he gave us yesterday. . . .

*(again, a reminder that you do the same)*

"Little children, when they're being taught to pray, are told to 'count their blessings' at the end of each day. We grow out of the habit, don't we, as we grow older? It's easy to turn into an old crab, something which could be avoided if we took just a little more time to thank God for all the good things of each day."

*(Collect pencils.)*

**DATE TRIED:**            **TIME:**            **REPEAT?:**

**RESULTS:**

# Advice Clinic

## EXPERIMENT NUMBER 10

**MATERIALS:** Small pieces of paper and pencils for all; empty container or box.

**CURRICULUM TIE-IN:** Problems of daily life; community.

**PREPARATION OF CLASS:** Usual. Also, ask for real honesty and sincerity in this experiment, noting that we are often thrown into contact with another person (as in this class) because we have some insight no one else can give him. ("I have no hands but yours," etc. . . .) Pass out pencils and paper.

"On the piece of paper please write, without signing it,
   either: a) some problem you have in growing up, for which
          you would like an answer, and which you wouldn't
          mind having read to the rest of the class,
   or b) some problem you think is common to many young
          people your age.

"You can disguise your handwriting if you like, and you might like
   to sign a pen name. . . .

(or something more interesting—a silly hat, six-pack holder, etc.)

"As you finish, I'll collect your questions in this box. . . .

"Now, let's read a few of the problems you've written, and maybe
   you'll be able to give some good advice to each other. . . .

(Read and discuss as time warrants, perhaps saving most to use in subsequent classes.)

"We've tried to help each other; would you stop with me now and ask God's help, help which is more powerful than any *we* can give? Is there anyone who would like to do that for us? . . .

*(Be ready with a two-liner in case no one offers.)*

*(If someone offered.)*

"Thank you, ............."

*(Collect pencils.)*

DATE TRIED:                    TIME:                    REPEAT?:

RESULTS:

# Doodle Prayer

**EXPERIMENT NUMBER 20**

**MATERIALS:** Paper and pencils for all.

**CURRICULUM TIE-IN:** Symbols and signs; God in everyday things.

**PREPARATION OF CLASS:** Usual. Pass out paper and pencils.

---

"Does anyone here doodle? . . . What does that mean? . . .

"Right. It's when you draw aimlessly, often while you're thinking about something else, or while you're talking on the phone. With your pencil and paper, try some doodling now. Don't try to draw a picture, just whatever comes to you in the way of designs or scribbles. . . .

*(Allow a couple of minutes, encourage class to keep at it. You doodle too.)*

"Next, I'm going to put some doodles on the board, and the funny thing about these doodles is that they can be 'triggers' for prayers. They started out as scribbles, and then took shape as prayer-reminders in someone's mind. See who can be the first to think up a prayer for this doodle. . . .

*(Draw this on the board.)*

"What does that seem to suggest? . . .

*(a knot, a tangle)*

"And how about a prayer based on it? . . .

*(If you just get ideas, collect them, and ask if anyone can shape them into a prayer. You may have to come up with something like "Lord, sometimes I feel like I'm tied in a knot. When that happens, please help me to remember you.")*

"And here's another one. See who can think up a prayer from this doodle. . . .

*(on the board)*

"Has anyone an idea? . . .

*(Possibly, "God, I'm going around in circles. Can you straighten me out?")*

"And here's a final doodle. Who can make up a prayer from this? . . .

"What does that suggest? . . .

*(a wall, a fortress)*

"Anyone for a prayer? . . .

*(Such as "Father, you're the wall of strength in our lives. Please don't let us forget that." Of course, these doodles could suggest several other prayers as well, any of which you'll happily accept.)*

"Now, look at the papers you doodled on. What do you see in your doodles that might lead to a prayer idea? . . . Whoever finds something can come up and draw it on the board. We'll see if we can guess what you have in mind. . . ."

(Reluctance may *mean* students are afraid they'll have to vocalize a prayer if they come up. You can assure them they need only share their doodles and ideas, that you will provide the prayer if no one else wants to. Be sure to stop before each prayer to ask the class to pray with the pray-er.)

"Why don't you all try this at home, and if you come up with anything good, bring it in for all of us?"

**DATE TRIED:**                **TIME:**                **REPEAT?:**


**RESULTS:**

## chapter 6
# PRAYERS WITH MUSIC

Bach to Rock, all sorts of music work and work very well in religion classrooms, especially in connection with prayer. Some teachers think, "Oh, my kids would never listen to classical music," and have eaten their words upon seeing the music of one of the masters seep into their boys and girls. Others can't stomach rock or jazz themselves, and so never take advantage of today's pop music as a trigger to praying.

Both records and cassette tapes are used to bring music into classrooms, the records having a slight edge on clarity and the tapes a slight edge on convenience and versatility. An investment in one or both is really worthwhile for any religion teacher or school.

Pop songs, widely used by teachers of many subjects today, present a pair of pitfalls we should be aware of. The first is the difficulty of keeping abreast of the new pop music. Rarely will a song be usable for even one year; you think you've found the perfect "prayer song" and use it with great success one year, only to be considered hopelessly dated when using it six months later. There are two ways around this difficulty.

One is to keep up with what's new as best you can through listening to the radio and asking students to bring in songs they think are suitable for prayer experiments. Every year will bring you one or two songs good enough to purchase on 45's, which are reasonable enough. Secondly, the very best songs you have collected over the years can be elevated to the status of "classics" and the class should be well aware that *you* know they are x-number of years old. Otherwise you'll be branded as antediluvian. If you've been on the pop song bandwagon for the past several years, you'll agree that many songs by the Beatles, Bob Dylan, Simon and Garfunkel, Judy Collins and —————— (fill in your favorite) are truly pop and/or folk classics, and will be as fine 20 years from now as they are today.

Another pitfall with classroom music is the danger of words not being understood when a record or tape is played, especially words sung with British accents. Song lyrics can be mimeographed and passed out (don't forget to collect them), a short song can be written on the board before class, words can be printed in wide marking pen on the pages of an easel-sized pad and held up before the whole class, or words can be typed to fit an opaque projector and shown on a screen. The small "toy" opaque projectors work very well, with a little practice, and have the advantages of being much more reasonable and much more portable than the large models.

(When the lights go out, however, and the teacher cleverly projects A Meaningful Song, will David, sitting by the door, try to escape? Tune in next week for the answer to this and other exciting questions. . . .)

If the words are so easily understood that no written words are necessary, or if the music is instrumental, you have the option of giving the class something to do while the music is playing or letting them "just sit." Sometimes "just sitting" is awkward and not particularly prayerful. What can you do with 25 young people listening to a record or tape?

Here are some suggestions:

—Ask the class to listen for the best line of the song and write it down for future reference.

—Ask them to draw or doodle whatever the music makes them feel.

—Line everyone up at the window to listen facing out (so they won't have to look at each other and giggle).

—Sit the class in a circle, facing outward (same reason).

—Ask them to listen with their heads on their desks or resting on their hands, or ask them to close their eyes.

The first two suggestions are usable for prayer experiments when the praying comes after the music; the last three work when the listening and praying occur simultaneously.

Most public libraries have good record collections, and a browse through them will often spark ideas for your own prayer experiments. The librarians are often receptive, also, to requests for particular purchases.

"Music hath charms . . . ," and we need all the charm we can get!

# The Song Without Music Prayer

**EXPERIMENT NUMBER 21**

**MATERIALS:** Words of a well-known (to your students) hymn; the folk hymns are very good, as are the traditional American shape-note folk hymns. At least one verse of the hymn should also be a good prayer. These can be handed out, or put on board or oversized paper, as described in Chapter 6. Possibly, a live performance or record of the hymn; or would your class be willing to sing it as a group?

**CURRICULUM TIE-IN:** Sacred music; whatever themes are in the hymn.

**VOCABULARY TO EXPLAIN:** Any words which might be difficult.

**PREPARATION OF CLASS:** If you happen to have a live singer(s), you will want to ask the audience to be gracious.

---

"How many know the hymn .......................................? . . .

"You've probably sung it in church—and how about in the shower? —many times. Let's listen to it now. . . .

*(if you plan a record or live performance)*

"Often, as we sing different hymns in church, we're struck by the beauty of their words. But we sing quickly, and are often distracted in church by interesting people sitting near us (among other things). Do you find this to be true? . . .

*(Have you one memory from your distant past of how you went to church primarily to see a Certain Someone, rather than to be with God? Most students find stories like this from their teacher's past delightfully wicked — and human.)*

95

"Let's take a closer look at this hymn, and use one verse of it as our prayer for this class. Which verse would make a good prayer? . . .

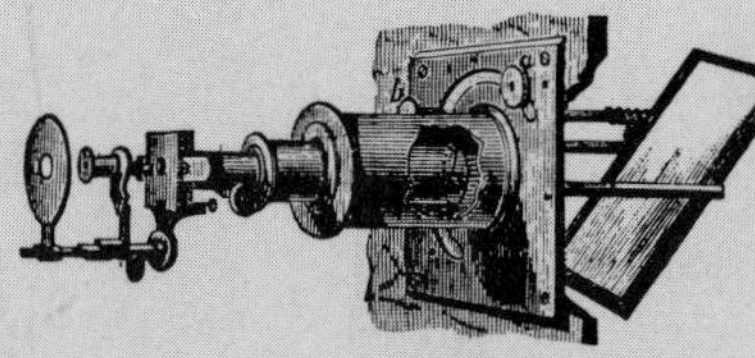

"O.K. Will you pray it with me now? Remember, reading words doesn't equal praying. We have to involve our hearts as well. . . .

*(Pray verse, slowly, not necessarily in the vocal pattern you would use to sing it.)*

"That was pretty good. You're getting to be good pray-ers! . . .

*(If by any stretch of the imagination you can say this truthfully, say it!)*

"It's a good idea to listen as carefully as we can to the words of the hymns we sing in church, rather than just reeling them off. A lot of them are really powerful, and we can pick out the verses of different hymns which work as prayers for us."

**DATE TRIED:**              **TIME:**              **REPEAT?:**

**RESULTS:**

# Top Ten Prayer

# EXPERIMENT NUMBER 22

**BACKGROUND:** Choose a song currently popular, or one of the pop songs you've promoted to a classic, which can double as a prayer. For example, in recent years songs like *The Long and Winding Road* (Beatles) and *Follow Me* (John Denver) can be understood as prayers if "you" is mentally changed to "You," and *Bridge Over Troubled Waters* (Simon and Garfunkel) makes sense as a prayer if "I" is understood to be God. A few phrases that don't jibe don't rule out the song; just ask the class to overlook them. Some "faith-rock" songs, of course, really are prayers already, and more of the old folk hymns, like *Amazing Grace*, are being recorded too. Any of these can be listened to, asking each student to try to make it *his* prayer. Others *lead* to prayer, as in the following example.

**MATERIALS:** Record or tape; words in some form (see Chapter 6), if needed.

**CURRICULUM TIE-IN:** Depends on song. (As an example, *I Don't Know How To Love Him* from *Jesus Christ Superstar* is used. Tie-ins would be conversion, adult faith, etc.)

**VOCABULARY TO EXPLAIN:** Depends on song.

**PREPARATION OF CLASS:** Usual.

---

"Today we're going to listen to a very familiar song, *I Don't Know How To Love Him* from *Jesus Christ Superstar*. How many know the song? . . .

*(Hand out words if you plan to.)*

"This has become a classic pop song, that is, one which will last and still be good listening many years from now. We're not going to listen from the viewpoint of the gospel story, or with reference to Mary Magdalene (who sings the song), but in a different way, a more personal way to see if this beautiful song can speak for us. Just in passing, though, what is the situation in the gospels where Mary and Jesus were concerned? . . .

*(hemming and hawing from students trying to work around the word "prostitute," at least junior high students)*

"Yes, she was a prostitute, a woman who had probably never known real love. Then she meets Jesus and is bowled over by the impact of him. . . .

(Euphemisms, in case the word bothers you: "lady of the evening," "woman of the streets"; ask yourself if this should bother you.)

"Her story, and her song, is the story of everyone who has ever been overpowered by Christ. . . . It's the story of a conversion of love. . . .

(Play song, keep silent a short while after; if you aren't uncomfortable with silences your class can learn not to be.)

"Mary sings, here, of being in love with God, which is not exactly the same as loving God. Her reaction is more mature, more adult. . . . So, overlooking the references she makes to her own life (about having 'so many men before' and so forth), let's listen to this song and see if it can be ours. We might wonder whether or not we will ever be in her place. When the song is over, we'll be quiet for half a minute, which is time you can use for prayer (maybe prayer about where *your* relationship with Jesus is going). . . .

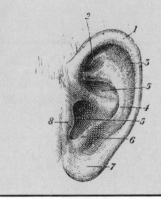

"Now, you might also keep your ears open for other songs, old and new, that can serve as prayers or lead to praying. A lot of students find this one of the best ways to pray. . . . What do you think?"

**DATE TRIED:**                **TIME:**                **REPEAT?:**

**RESULTS:**

# Opera Prayer

## EXPERIMENT NUMBER 20

**BACKGROUND:** Most students will probably protest when you announce an "opera prayer," and yet, the dramatic stories and human passions of most operas make them naturals for young people—and also good lead-ins to praying. We don't always have to limit ourselves to the familiar. What's more, the occasional student who is into classical music will appreciate your recognition of his tastes (even if he wouldn't reveal them to the class).

**MATERIALS:** Some short operatic scene (two minutes or so) on record or tape. The example used here is part of the Nile Scene, in Act III, of Giuseppe Verdi's *Aida*. Other familiar scenes you might use are:

> Puccini's *Tosca*: the torture scene from Act II.
> Verdi's *Otello*: the murder of Desdemona in Act IV.
> Poulenc's *Dialogue of the Carmelities*: the guillotining of the nuns in the final scene.
> Or, if you'd like a seduction scene, the end of Act III of Gounod's *Faust,* complete with pointy-tailed devil.

Notice that these are all rather lurid selections, just the sort of thing to catch the fancy of the horror-movie fans we teach. French, Italian or Russian opera are likely to be more easily appreciated than most German, or even English, operas; the former have, as a rule, many appealing melodies.

**CURRICULUM TIE-IN:** Depends on what you've chosen. In this example: loyalty, trust, betrayal.

**PREPARATION OF CLASS:** Usual, plus any pep talk you may think necessary on the beauties of classical music.

"Today we're going to have a musical prayer, and the music is going to be from a famous opera. Does anyone know the story of Verdi's *Aida? . . .*

99

"Well, it's a very famous opera, written in 1871 by the great Italian composer Giuseppe Verdi. He wrote it for the Viceroy of Egypt, who wanted to celebrate the opening of a new opera house in Cairo with an opera about ancient Egypt. Verdi told a story of war between Egypt and Ethiopia in the time of the Pharaohs. What Old Testament people do we associate with the Pharaohs? . . .

*(Joseph, Moses)*

*(Give whatever details of plot you think the traffic can bear.)*

"We're going to listen to a few minutes of a scene between the Ethiopian princess, Aida, who has been captured and is slave to the daughter of the Pharaoh, and her father, the king of Ethiopia. He wants Aida to get her boyfriend, who happens to be the captain of the Egyptian guard, to give away a military secret so the Ethiopian army can catch the Egyptian army.

"Aida, then, is caught between two conflicting loyalties, one to her country and her father, and one to the man she loves. Let's listen and hear the two of them. The language is Italian. . . .

*(You will have located earlier the spot on the record where you wish to pick up the singing. If you think exact details of what is being sung are necessary, you can brief the class on these.)*

"How do you feel about this young lady's problem? . . . What would you do if you were Aida? . . .

"Have you ever been in such a situation yourself, where you didn't know how to choose between two people or two causes? . . .

*(Do you have an example from your life? One of the class will probably come up with the common conflict between values of parents and values of friends.)*

"This business of being caught in the middle can happen in anyone's life. We probably won't be faced with betraying whole armies, like Aida was, but the chances are that we'll have to face similar choices more than once in our lives. At any rate, when this does happen, we'll need God's help. Could anyone, finally, give us a prayer about such times of conflict that may lie ahead for any or all of us? . . .

(If no one offers) "Let's see if I can think of the right words. Will you pray with me? 'Lord, like the girl in the opera, we all will have times coming up when we seem to be asked to make impossible choices. When these come, please help us remember to turn to you, and please help us to make the right choice.'

"That wasn't so hard, was it? . . ."

**DATE TRIED:**          **TIME:**          **REPEAT?:**

**RESULTS:**

# "Superstar" Prayer

## EXPERIMENT NUMBER 24

**BACKGROUND:** Whatever you, personally, feel about *Jesus Christ Superstar,* it surely must be judged thought-provoking. This experiment avoids the controversial aspects of *Superstar,* making use of it as a prayer-starter. Your use of the rock opera for other purposes is quite another matter. Have you seen *Jesus Christ Superstar: A Guide for Religious Educators* by Landry, Onley and Wise (Cincinnati: North American Liturgy Resources, 1971. $2.95)? The music of *Godspell* can be used in prayer experiments in a similar way.

**MATERIALS:** Record or tape of one of the *Superstar* songs or sections. The example given here is "This Jesus Must Die" from side one of the album. Also, words to pass out or project, unless your record or tape is *very* clear; bible marked to John 12:12-19.

**CURRICULUM TIE-IN:** Jesus, Holy Week, sacred music.

**VOCABULARY TO EXPLAIN:** Pharisees, Caiaphas, Annas.

**PREPARATION OF CLASS:** Usual, plus any general discussion of *Jesus Christ Superstar* you feel necessary. How familiar are students with this work? What do they think of it? Do they think it will be lasting music, listened to year after year, or was it just a fad?

"Today we are going to play and think about a portion of *Jesus Christ Superstar* for our prayer experiment. The section is 'This Jesus Must Die,' which is the passage where the high priests try to decide what to do about Jesus.

"Let's set the background for this scene first. Who knows something about it? . . . What was the situation? . . .

*(Jesus had entered Jerusalem on Palm Sunday, to much acclaim.)*

"Who'd like to read what the bible says about it? . . .

(Jn 12: 12-19)

"Notice, in the last verse, the Pharisees are worried. Who are they? . . .

*(super-strict Jewish sect, famous for observing the letter of the law)*

"In the opera, we have Caiaphas and Annas as well. Who were they? . . .

*(Caiaphas — high priest of the Jews; Annas—his father-in-law and former high priest)*

"Let's listen. . .

*(Play record or tape.)*

"We've been listening to characters (who were real people, of course) plotting against Jesus. They're disturbed because he seems to be a threat to them. I'd like to ask you now to think, and then pray, about the same thing. Have you ever tried to think how you could hurt, or even get rid of, anyone who seemed a threat to you? . . . Would anyone be willing to give us an example of this today, perhaps *not* from his own life? . . .

*(How about rivals for affection, both at home and in peer groups?)*

"Let's take half a minute and talk to God about this problem of feeling threatened by others, especially if it's a problem we've had in our own life. That will be our prayer for today. . . .

*(Silence can seem endless, but it's a beautiful thing for students to get used to; your example of easiness during silence helps.)*

103

"As we learn more and more about Jesus, we see how much his life had in common with our lives. He experienced the same feelings we do; he had the same things happen to him that we have happen to us. The gap of two thousand years between Jesus and us is really only one of clothing and customs and culture, not one of feeling or humanness. Christians, believing this, also believe that Jesus understands and can have meaning for men of all times."

**DATE TRIED:**                    **TIME:**                    **REPEAT?:**

**RESULTS:**

# Pick-a-Thought Prayer

**EXPERIMENT NUMBER 25**

**MATERIALS:** One- to two-minute (no longer) record or tape of instrumental music—something calm (classical, semiclassical, oriental, etc.). Don't pick an instrumental version of a song with well-known words, for the mind has a tendency to supply the words in such music.

**CURRICULUM TIE-IN:** Power of good example; thanksgiving.

**PREPARATION OF CLASS:** Usual.

---

"All through our lives we meet people who affect us so much that we can say our lives have been changed for better by them. Now I'd like you to think of someone you know—anyone at all—who has had a great influence for good on you. . . .

*(The thought given here is one of many; how about, instead, "something you're sorry for," "someone who needs help," etc.?)*

*(Wait 30 seconds.)*

"Now I'm going to play some music, about a minute long. When it starts, think about the person you've chosen and what he or she means to you and your life. Try to picture this person. Picture him or her doing whatever he or she has done for you. Halfway through the music I'll signal you by tapping on the desk with a pencil. At that point, until the music ends, see if you can make up a prayer inside you thanking God for letting this person come into your life, AND maybe asking, if you like, for the gift for yourself of being this sort of person, a person who can make a lasting difference to others. Any questions? . . .

*(or ringing a bell, or making a mark on the board, or. . .)*

"O.K., here we go. . . .

*(Play music; halfway through give signal.)*

"Would anyone care to tell us whether or not this sort of praying works for him? . . . This is something you might want to try again at home, using all sorts of thoughts you've picked out, such as ................................... . . ."

*(See examples above.)*

**DATE TRIED:**                    **TIME:**                    **REPEAT?:**

**RESULTS:**

# "This Is Your Life" in Music

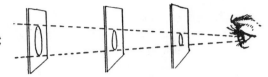

## EXPERIMENT NUMBER 26

**BACKGROUND:** This theme, tracing one's life from its beginning to its imaginary ending, is repeated twice more in Experiments No. 33 and No. 39. Hopefully, such repetition of this essential thought will help each student focus attention on the quality of his life span, and give perspective to his view of each day of that life.

**MATERIALS:** Instrumental music of your choice, on record or tape, about two minutes long. Choose a piece of music which divides easily into four sections, which will represent childhood, youth, adulthood, and old age (and if your music has more sections, subdivide these age categories and/or use the final section of music for the prayer itself). Some versions of the theme music from *Gone With the Wind* work very well.

**CURRICULUM TIE-IN:** Purpose of life; death; vocation, the future.

**PREPARATION OF CLASS:** Usual.

---

"Today we're going to try to retrace our lives up until now, and then see if we can imagine what our futures will be like. I have some music, and it has four sections to it. Each of these sections can represent one phase of our life here on earth:
　　1 — our babyhood and childhood
　　2 — our years as teenagers
　　3 — our grown-up years
　　4 — our old age, assuming we last that long.

*(Write numbers and phases of life on board.)*

"When I start the music, will you try this? . . . Sit very still and see if you can think over the years that have passed, your childhood, trying to remember what it was like to be little and some of the things you did.

107

"When the second part of the music starts, I'll put a circle around the '2' on the board so you'll know we've reached that point. Then, think about what your life is like now, during the years you're in your teens. Especially, try to look at your life as though you were a stranger to it, an outsider who is viewing *your* life from up on a cloud or through a telescope. No, this won't be easy. . . .

"I'll circle the '3' when that section of the music starts, and you might try to imagine what sort of life you'll lead as an adult, and at '4,' how you'll be as an old person. Finally, the hardest part of all, when you sense that the end of the music is approaching, imagine that the end of your life has come.

"After the music finishes, we'll keep still for a half-minute or so, and see if we feel like saying anything inside ourselves to God, who's given us this life and is with us all the way through it. Does anyone have any questions? . . .

*(Perhaps your music works out so that you have a tail end suitable for the prayer time; just be sure that the "death music" is suitable for dying.)*

*(Play music, and don't forget to circle the numbers on the board at the right times. If you are obviously trying to think about your life while the music is playing, rather than watching your students, they'll find it easier to follow suit. Allow for prayer time afterward.)*

"And that's a look at our lives for today. I wonder if there's anyone who would be willing to tell us how this experiment worked out for him? . . . Would something like this be easier to do when you're alone? . . ."

**DATE TRIED:**  **TIME:**  **REPEAT?:**

**RESULTS:**

# chapter 7
# MEDITATIONS

Meditations are both the most interesting prayer experiments for most students and the most difficult. Interesting, because they challenge creativity and are fun; difficult, because they take longer and require a seriousness and self-discipline not all students have.

For this reason, before each meditation it's a good idea to point out that meditations are only for the more mature student—and, perhaps, that it's a compliment to the class that their teacher believes they can tackle a meditation (teacher as con artist again?).

Take a few more seconds than usual to get everyone settled for the prayer time; ask the students to close their eyes (no peeking) and get comfortable, then be prepared for anything up to and including bodies stretched out on the floor! If you don't care for bodies on the floor of your classroom, decide (in advance) your limits on "being comfortable" and tell the class how far they can go. Explain that being still aids one's powers of concentration.

Candles in a dark room are a perfect aid for this type of prayer experiment, which is well enhanced by a little atmosphere. A calm, slow voice helps too, yet a voice with the expression of a good storyteller. Some of the meditations suggest music, which is optional but very helpful if you can arrange it. Use what you are able to put your hands on. See what other sound effects you can create.

Meditations are attempts at the second sort of prayer we discussed in Chapter 1: attempts to create a setting where all allow themselves to be quieted—first in body, then in soul—consciously trying to place themselves in the presence of God and be open to him. This may, or may not, facilitate the two-way communication we have defined as prayer; the only way to know is to try some of the experiments. Meditations may take a little time to get used to, so expect the first try to be less than perfect.

An occasional student (usually a very pragmatic, mechanically oriented boy) may reject this sort of praying completely. He or she should certainly feel free to do so. Tell the students that anyone who just isn't grabbed by meditations after a couple of tries can tune out for the few minutes they take. This is also a good reason for varying from class to class the type of prayer experiment used.

We have two kinds of meditations in this book; there probably are several more types waiting to be created.

# "You Are There" Meditations

For centuries, books on praying have suggested that the pray-er imagine he's back in some biblical setting. The classic story is of the pious nun who took herself back imaginarily to the Last Supper, as pictured by Leonardo. Her meditation was a complete flop because, instead of being able to concentrate on Jesus and his words, she found herself thoroughly distracted by the thought that he would catch cold sitting before the open doorway. The Rosary is probably the original "You Are There" meditation. In our day, the "You Are There" idea is familiar from both the radio and TV history programs of that name.

In these meditations we try to take ourselves mentally to some time and place where we might have found it simple to encounter God. However, we should also make it clear to our students, abundantly clear, that the best of all places to find God is not in daydreams or make-believe worlds, but in the people and places of our very real, everyday lives.

# Early Christians' Meditation

**BACKGROUND:** Any time or incident in church history can be turned into a "You Are There" meditation. You might check on what your students are studying in history; a group studying renaissance England could go to the Tower with St. Thomas More, and European history survey students could be with Columbus in 1492.

**MATERIALS:** None necessary, but candles helpful. Have you any pictures of ancient Rome or the catacombs? Could you possibly hold this part of the class in some crypt-like spot in your church or school?

**CURRICULUM TIE-IN:** Early church history; martyrdom, death.

**VOCABULARY TO EXPLAIN:** Catacombs (if necessary).

**PREPARATION OF CLASS:** Usual.

"This experiment is going to take us back many years to ancient Rome, the Rome of the emperors. Does anyone know something about this time? Can you fill us in on, say, dates? . . .

*(31 B.C.-late 400's A.D.)*

"How about clothes? . . .

*(tunics, togas, sandals)*

"And worship? . . .

*(pagan; many gods until Constantine made Christianity the official religion in 325 A.D.)*

113

"And what was ancient Rome famous for? . . .

*(military conquests, law, gladiatorial contests, Caesar(s), roads, etc.)*

"What connection is there between Jesus and the Roman Empire? . . .

*(Palestine was under Roman rule when Christ lived there.)*

"How many have seen movies about ancient Rome? . . .

*(Don't let class get carried away describing movie plots in detail; the Ben Hur chariot race can eat up 15 minutes.)*

"That's very good. Now, let's close our eyes and relax, and try something. See how well you can do with this meditation. We're going to pretend we're back in ancient Rome, during the rule of the emperor Nero. Nero was, unfortunately, a very poor ruler and a very wicked man, who ruled Rome from 54 to 68 A.D. This would be about 20 years after the death of Jesus.

"Nero killed his mother and he killed his wife, and he used the small group of Christians in Rome as a scapegoat, someone to blame for the city's problems—as Hitler blamed the Jews in Germany for many of his problems.

*(You can add or substract from these details of Roman history, but don't assume that any students have much of a background even if they have "learned" these facts in school. "Learned facts" have a way of evaporating as soon as they've been put on a test paper. Our source on the Roman Christians during the reign of Nero is Tacitus' Annals, Book XV.)*

114

"Let's imagine that we're part of the Christian community in Rome when Nero was emperor. First, imagine how you might be dressed . . . and the sort of house you might live in . . . . Do you belong to a wealthy, noble Roman family, or are you the child of slaves? . . .

"Our small band of Christians has to meet in secret, because our religion is outlawed. It's dangerous to be a Christian, but ever since the two great men from the Holy Land—Peter and Paul—spoke to us, we've been more sure than ever that we wanted to risk all to follow Jesus.

"We have to meet in the catacombs, hidden chambers under the earth scattered all over Rome. Ours is outside the city, on the Appian Way, and that's where we are now. Can you feel how damp it is down here? . . . Can you see the candles flickering in the dark? . . . Can you hear the underground streams trickling near you? . . .

*(Can you make your voice catacomb-y?)*

"We're all here for Mass, which has just been offered. Each of us has come at the risk of his life, and now the members of the community embrace and prepare to leave. Your parents are next to you. . . .

"A few leave at a time, praying they won't be seen by anyone outside. Soon you follow your father up the narrow flight of steps cut out of the earth, with your mother behind. . . .

"As you get to the top, you're suddenly grabbed from behind . . . a hand is clapped over your mouth to keep you from making any noise . . . you see the same thing happening to your parents . . . the emperor's soldiers have discovered your meeting place and are capturing all of your group. . . .

*(appropriate change in voice, without lapsing into melodrama)*

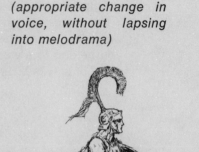

"Your heart is pounding. . . You see everyone gagged and tied up and dragged to a cart. . . you're dumped in the cart. . . it moves off, over the bumpy stones of the Appian Way, and you realize you're heading back to Rome. . . .

"Without a doubt, you know that you're headed for the dungeons under one of the Roman arenas. . . .

*(You can stop here, or actually herd your Christians into an arena—or even Nero's gardens—to face salivating lions or be used as human torches; Nero and his empress can preside if you like. How far you go depends on many variables, such as time, the age and behavior of your class, how well things are going up to this point, and so forth.)*

"While in the cart riding back to Rome in the darkness, let's try to do a very difficult thing. This will require imagination. Let's pause and try to imagine what we would say to God at this point. . . .

"Now, finally, we're going to leave ancient Rome and come back to present-day America, where we don't have to worry about worshiping freely. Can you get yourself across about 2,000 years? . . .

*(Make the transition easily, not abruptly.)*

"Well, would anyone like to describe his trip for us, his feelings? . . ."

**DATE TRIED:**                    **TIME:**                    **REPEAT?:**

**RESULTS:**

# Castle Meditation

**EXPERIMENT NUMBER 20**

**MATERIALS:** Optional, but helpful  Gregorian chant record or tape (or any plainchant); picture of castle (or a few turrets drawn on chalkboard).  Try travel bureaus for castle posters.  Candles are good for this experiment; it can also be done with slides of castle and surrounding landscape.

**CURRICULUM TIE-IN:** Medieval Church history (Crusades, etc.); Mass, Eucharist; sacred music.

**VOCABULARY TO EXPLAIN:** (for young children) knights, Crusades.

**PREPARATION OF CLASS:** Usual.

---

"Today we're going to take a trip back to the Middle Ages.  When was that? . . . What do you know about that time? . . . With what continent do you associate these things? . . .

*(c. 900-1300 A.D.)*
*(feudal system, knighthood, cathedrals, etc.)*
*(Europe)*

"If you had lived then, it might have been in a house like this. . . .

*(Show castle picture.)*

"Please get comfortable now and close your eyes.  Let's pretend that we're back in the Middle Ages.  You are a knight, on (of course) a milk-white steed.  Can you give your horse a name? . . . You've been away on a Crusade to the Holy Land for five long years. . . .

*(Close eyes unless you're using slides, of course.)*

*(Dare you try hoofbeats? With a silly class, no.)*

"Finally after being captured, tortured, and having escaped by being lowered over a city wall in a basket (like St. Paul almost 1000 years before you), you have made your way back to your country, back to your village, and finally, to your castle. You stop before the castle walls. Here it is, at last, the place you've dreamed of all these years. . . .

"What has happened since you've been gone? Is your lady alive or dead from the Plague? And your children, how are they, especially your oldest son who was just four and learning to ride when you left? Will they even know you? . . .

"Your tired horse, not the fine animal he once was but still your most faithful friend, walks over the drawbridge, enters the courtyard, and you look up at the turrets of your castle sparkling in the sun. . . .

"From the highest tower, up where the chapel is, comes beautiful music, the music of the Mass. You slide off your horse. You go through the big arched doorway and slowly make your way to the tower part of the castle. . . .

*(If using music, play softly, talking over it.)*

"Picture yourself walking up the spiral staircase of the tower, to the very top where the chapel is. You haven't been at Mass for five years, for the chaplain of your Crusade died just after your ship left Italy. You long to see your family, who are probably inside the chapel. And you also long to worship God as you once did and be able to receive Holy Communion again. . . .

"You pause at the door of the chapel. Take a moment now and tell God what's in your heart. . . .

*(about 30 seconds' silence or music)*

119

"And now you go in. . . . What do you find? . . .

*(about 30 seconds more of silence or music)*

"Now we're going to come back to 19—. The next time you go to church you might try to remember how you felt about the Mass when you were a Crusader, the Mass we take so much for granted because it's so available to us. . . .

*(Allow a few seconds to "wake up"—hope that you won't have to wake anyone up literally.)*

"Would anyone like to share his feelings with us when he was outside the chapel door, or tell us what he found when he went inside? . . ."

*(good starting point for a longer "ferverino" on appreciating Mass and Communion)*

**DATE TRIED:**                    **TIME:**                    **REPEAT?:**

**RESULTS:**

# Soap Opera Meditation

EXPERIMENT NUMBER

**BACKGROUND:** This experiment walks a rather thin line between farce and seriousness, encompassing both. Although this makes it difficult to pull off, and also indicates that you should do a little rehearsing on your own in advance, students are delighted to see that something as serious as religion can be woven into a silly situation. If you're very spirit-filled yourself and/or have an exceptionally fine class, this can be role-played, with students acting out the episodes.

**MATERIALS:** None. However, if you can get organ music like "soapers" use on TV, to play at the appropriate spots, fine. You could tape it from TV. Or, consider humming a few schmaltzy bars here and there.

**CURRICULUM TIE-IN:** People, human problems of daily life.

**PREPARATION OF CLASS:** Usual, plus a special request for seriousness of purpose. Sometimes a remark like "I'd only try this with a class which had proved it was mature" helps (and sometimes it doesn't).

---

"How many have ever watched soap operas on TV? . . .

*(Name favorites.)*

"In the better ones, the people seem normal enough, don't they? It's just what happens to them that's unreal; they go from murder trials to major illnesses to. . . .

*(Let class describe, but not get too long-winded.)*

"We're going to make up our own soap operas today. I'm going to split the class in half, and give each group a character. The groups will have two minutes to decide some of the details of this person's life and we'll take it from there. . . .

*(Divide class. With less than 20 students, you may prefer to operate as one group.)*

121

"Now, group 1, your character is a boy about your age. He is close to God—this is important. Decide together on a name for him, where he lives, what his family's like, what he looks like, and any other details you care to add. . . .

(Allow two minutes or so.)

"And, group 2, your character is a girl, about your age. She is close to God—don't forget this. Can you decide on the same things for her? . . .

"Now, we're going to make up a soap-opera type story about each of these characters. In group 1, who'll give us the background you made up about the young man? . . .

(Be prepared for anything to happen to this character, but remember that you have veto power if "his life" seems to be getting out of hand. You may have to guide the shape of the story toward a final dilemma.)

"Good. Now let's go around group 1, one at a time. Each person will add some action on to the story of this boy, as in a soap opera. The idea is that by the time the last person adds on his piece of the story, your hero must be in some real mess. . . .

"Here's the hard part. Remember, this is a prayer experiment, a meditation, in fact. Let's all stop here, sit back comfortably in our chairs and get in a prayerful frame of mind. Why not close your eyes and see if you can do the experiment part, which comes next? . . .

"We've gotten this young man into a terrible spot. . . . Remember too that he's a person who is close to God. Those of you who think you can do it, will you try to put yourself in this boy's place and make up a prayer—inside yourself—that might be *his* prayer at this point in his life? . . .

*(Describe his predicament very seriously.)*

*(This is the only prayer experiment in which we ask students to pray as someone else would, rather than as themselves. The point of this is that those still not at ease with prayer for themselves may very well get the feel of spontaneous prayer when asked to imagine how someone else might pray.)*

"And now, group 2, let's try the same thing with the young lady you've created. . . .

*(Repeat group 1 directions.)*

"This is a somewhat off-beat type of prayer experiment, and not an easy one. How many felt they could enter into someone else's skin and pray as he or she would? . . ."

**DATE TRIED:**                    **TIME:**                    **REPEAT?:**

**RESULTS:**

123

# Jungle Meditation

**EXPERIMENT NUMBER 30**

**MATERIALS:** Most effective with African religious music, or just African music, if you can get it. Suggested: the *Kyrie* from the famous *Missa Luba,* the Congolese Mass. Candles are good, and you might add some "jungle scenery"; a houseplant to stand for tropical greenery, a tiger's face or eyes on the board.

**CURRICULUM TIE-IN:** Faith; martyrdom, death; sacred music; missions.

**VOCABULARY TO EXPLAIN:** If using the *Missa Luba,* "Kyrie Eleison" and "Christe Eleison" ("Lord, have mercy" and "Christ, have mercy").

**PREPARATION OF CLASS:** Usual.

"This is an imaginary story, but it's based on truth. Today we're going to travel to the heart of Africa. The music I'm about to play is music of African Christians, written to praise God in their traditional style. While it's playing, will you settle back, close your eyes and see if you can imagine you're in Africa, and that you're a black African Christian worshiping in your chapel in the jungle. . . .

"Since Jesus has come into your life, through the teaching of a missionary from America, your life has changed. You've become a Christian, and for the first time in your life you know why you're here on earth. You've become a person with inner peace, and you wish all your people could share this love he's brought you. Now you're leaving your little chapel. It's in a clearing in the jungle. Look back at it. . . . What does it look like? . . .

*(If you can't find religious music, use non-religious —if possible—and say the worshipers have just left the chapel.)*

"The only time the missionary could come to the chapel was after supper today, and he only comes every two months. Of course, you wanted to be there when he came so you walked to this spot from your village, four miles away. There he goes, off on his donkey, in the other direction. . . . The other worshipers live on his route and are following him. . . . You're left alone. . . .

"You go toward your home, through the jungle, still feeling filled with joy. It's getting quite dark, and quickly. . . .

*(How about a jungly voice?)*

"Can you hear the jungle animals settling down for the night? . . . There are birds flying above you, and monkeys still swinging in the trees overhead. . . . Noises of larger animals are on both sides of you. . . . Something is slithering in the tree to your right. . . .

"Night falls very fast in the jungle. It's pitch black already, and you're moving through the trees by instinct, as you've done since you were a child. . . .

"Suddenly, you stop. . . . Was that the noise of human feet up ahead? . . . or was it in back of you? . . .

"Now it's quiet again, and you move on even more quickly. . . .

"Suddenly, without any warning at all, you're surrounded by about ten of the men of your village, armed with spears. Can you see them? . . . They don't seem friendly. . . . They take your arms and march you the rest of the way home. . . . None of them will answer your questions as to why they're here. . . .

"Finally, you reach your village. A fire is lit, and around it sits the entire population of the tribe, including your parents. . . .

"Standing in front of the fire is the witch doctor, who is the medicine man and real leader of the village. He conducts the religious ceremonies of the tribe, which include animal sacrifice. . . . Can you see how he's dressed? . . . his mask? . . .

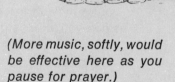

"He says to you, 'You have given up the religion of your ancestors. The penalty for that is torture and death. We will give you one minute to decide whether or not you will renounce your new religion, this Christianity, and return to our old ways.' Which will it be? . . .

"You are terrified. What shall you do? . . . or say? . . . You know you have to talk to God about this. What do you say to him? . . .

*(More music, softly, would be effective here as you pause for prayer.)*

"Fortunately, we're going to leave the jungle before this story continues, and come back to our classroom. This wasn't completely a make-believe trip. Many, many Christians in what we call mission lands—Africa, the far East, the Indies—have died because they chose Christianity over their more primitive religions. In Uganda, in 1886, for instance, 20 young boys were tied in bundles of straw and burned because they would not give up their new Christian faith.

"Now that we're home again, would anyone like to share his thoughts or his prayers with us? . . . If you were going to try this prayer experiment with younger children, what would you add to it, or take away? . . ."

*(Once students get used to meditations like this one, they are in a position to visit classes of younger children and try the same experiments with them. You might see if some other teacher would like to have one of your students visit; it's a very good experience for both younger and older kids.)*

**DATE TRIED:**            **TIME:**            **REPEAT?:**

**RESULTS:**

# Heaven Meditation

**BACKGROUND:** This, obviously, could be expanded into an hour-long class, with the prayer experiment to wrap it up. Some readers may note how theologically unsophisticated this experiment is. Well, yes—and so are our students.

## EXPERIMENT NUMBER 31

**MATERIALS:** Optional, but helpful: "heavenly" music (record or tape of choir or orchestra, or autoharp to strum); stars hanging on thread from ceiling or drawn on blackboard; non-messy goodies to pass out; spray can of floral air freshener (lemon is a nice scent, not too cloying) or incense if you can stand it; someone or a tape to be "voice at heaven's gates" saying, "Welcome, we've been waiting for you," or something like that. Candles are good for this experiment; it can be done with slides.

**CURRICULUM TIE-IN:** Heaven, eternity; hope, joy, presence of God.

**PREPARATION OF CLASS:** Usual.

---

"We're going to take a trip today (no, not that kind of trip). Look at these stars. Can you guess where we're going? . . .

*(if you use stars)*

"That's right, we're going to heaven. And since that's a happy place to be, I thought it might help us get in the mood if we had something good to eat. . . .

*(Pass out goodies yourself, if you have them.)*

"What's heaven like? Do we really know? . . . These are all good guesses. The bible doesn't really tell us too much about heaven, just that there *is* a heaven. St. John wrote about rainbows and jewels and a 'sea that seemed to be made of glass-like crystal.' Jesus compared heaven to a wedding feast, and in his day wedding feasts were blasts. And St. Paul told us that 'no eye has seen and no ear heard . . . all

*(Expect answers about clouds, harps, wings, etc.)*

*(Rv 4:3-6)*

*(Mt 22: 1-14)*

that God has prepared for those who love him.' Some people think heaven will be earth, without any faults. Just, now, we can only use our imaginations and our earthly senses to guess at what wonderful things are ahead of us.

*(I Cor 2, 9)*

"Now, please get comfortable and close your eyes. Let's pretend we've dropped dead somewhere and have arrived at heaven. . . .

*(Welcoming voice if you have one—or your own.)*

"What does it look like in heaven? . . . Is it a green meadow with flowers (like the poppy field in *The Wizard of Oz)*? . . . Is it a jeweled palace? . . . or is it like your own home, but without any clutter, or dirty dishes, or arguments?. . .

"What does it sound like? . . . Are there really harps strumming? . . . an orchestra playing? . . . a rock band so everyone can dance? (can souls dance without bodies?) . . . and who is there? . . .

*(Play music if you have any.)*

"And what does it smell like? . . . a candy factory? (making candy that won't cause cavities, of course, if souls have teeth) . . . a pizza house? . . . a field of flowers? . . .

*(Spray floral air spray if you have it, over heads, not in faces.)*

"Anyway, here you are in heaven, walking around—or are you floating? or flying? . . . What *are* you doing? . . . Think of the things you like to do most of all here on earth (like swimming, or sleeping outside in the summer). . . .

*(Choose suitable examples for your class.)*

*(Someone's bound to snicker here; you can say "yes, all the good things of earth.")*

"And think, too, of the happiest moments of your life so far (moments with a pet, perhaps, or coming home after you've been away). . . .

(As in all teaching, know your kids — some may have horrible homes to come home to; choose examples that won't hurt.)

"And now, try to multiply the joy these things bring you by ten thousand. Maybe this begins to approach what it's like to be in heaven. . . .

"We are told that the greatest joy of heaven will be seeing God (the Beatific Vision, it's called). Can you imagine now that here in heaven God is with you constantly? . . . How do you feel? . . . Let's take a minute to imagine what it's really like to be in his presence. . . .

"Now we're going to come back to earth. The best thing of all is that we don't have to leave God behind in heaven. You know that we're all in his presence all day, every day, right here on earth. In fact, this is where heaven starts.

"And this hasn't really been a make-believe trip like our trips to the jungle or the Middle Ages, because someday each of us will have a chance to make this trip. Will you be ready for it? . . ."

*(if you've done these)*

*(If lights are out, turn on gradually so "spell" isn't broken too quickly.)*

**DATE TRIED:**            **TIME:**            **REPEAT?:**

**RESULTS:**

# Wild Party Meditation

## EXPERIMENT NUMBER 32

**BACKGROUND:** Religion teachers seem to run the gamut from super-relevant (those who concentrate almost exclusively on the here-and-now) to completely irrelevant (those so deeply into theology and scripture they never touch the lives of their students). Somewhere in between is probably about right, although we must each find our own style. This here-and-and-now meditation could lead to an entire class on morality today, so before using it you'd want to get your own thoughts together.

**MATERIALS:** Record or tape of some pop music, suitable for playing at a teen-age party. You can omit this, however. If you want to carry out the party idea further, how about food?

**CURRICULUM TIE-IN:** Morality, dating, love; problems of daily life; presence of God.

**PREPARATION OF CLASS:** Usual.

---

"Today we have another meditation, a little different from our others. This prayer experiment is going to take us to a party, a really good one. . . .

*(Pass out food, if any.)*

"Now, if everyone will get settled and relaxed, we'll begin. This will probably work better if you close your eyes. Think what a good party is like. . . . You're with someone you like (very much). . . . Is it formal or informal? . . . What are you wearing? . . . Are the parents of the kid giving the party at home? . . . Has anyone brought a bottle? . . . Who's smoking what? . . . Someone's telling a pretty sick story. . . .

*(three guesses as to where the parents are)*

"You're with ......................—fill in your favorite name. . . . You're having a good time, and you notice that the lights are gradually being turned off. Things are getting quieter. . . . Couples are drifting off to various parts of the house. . . . Picture it. . . .

*(Let each go as far as he wants to in his imagination, rather than attempting to describe a party suitable both for your innocent students and those older than Eve.)*

"One of you is probably thinking, How is anyone going to drag God into this? Here's how. . . .

"If our religion is at the core of our life, and if it touches everything we do—even situations like this (especially situations like this), then God is as present at the party as he is in church. I'm going to put on some music that's playing at the party, and I wonder if, while it's playing, you would try to talk to God about what he has to do with this occasion. . . . Maybe you'll decide you don't want him there. . . .

*(if you have music)*

*(Play about a minute of music.)*

"This wasn't such an easy experiment, was it? Let's leave the party now, and come back here. Would anyone be willing to share his thoughts on this with us? . . . Let me ask, first, if you can pray along with music like that we just heard? . . ."

*(Caution: this, obviously, is a very open-ended experiment and you don't want the kids to feel manipulated into coming up with your answers. Please let them feel free to express themselves, and don't come glomming down on them with a "sin" lecture. You may never agree on how the situation should be handled, or how God fits into it, although we can hope all Christians would O.K. the principle of respect for others—at all times, in all places—because each is a child of God.)*

**DATE TRIED:**                **TIME:**              **REPEAT?:**

**RESULTS:**

# Yoga-Type Meditations

Yoga, the ancient practice of India, is often misunderstood. Not a religion, yogas (for there are different types) are methods of physical, mental and spiritual development designed for people of all—or no—faiths. The goal of yoga, which means "union," is the uniting of the individual soul with the soul of the universe. Believers, naturally, read "God" for "soul of the universe," and yoga students often become living examples of men filled with the "peace which passes all understanding," men whose lives are in union with God.

Many teachers and books on yoga suggest ideas for meditation, ideas which correspond to the teaching of Jesus to "seek first the kingdom of God within." All we have done is "baptized" some of these ideas for our classroom purposes, by making them refer specifically to God. What is implicit in yoga, the awareness of God, we have spelled out explicitly so that these meditations can serve as vehicles for prayer.

The study of yoga, both physical (Hatha Yoga) and mental (which has many forms, one being the rapidly spreading practice of transcendental meditation), is one with rich dividends for religion teachers. It can be a means of personal growth and "greening." It can also shed much light both on the spirit common to all world religions and on the approach of today's young people to the spiritual. A fine book synthesizing yoga and Christianity is *Christian Yoga* by J. M. Dechanet, O.S.B. (New York, Harper & Row, 1960. $3.75). *The New Religions,* by Jacob Needleman (New York, Pocket Books, 1972. $1.25) also offers fascinating insights, as does the later work of Thomas Merton on the meeting of Eastern and Western spirituality.

133

# "This Is Your Life" Meditation

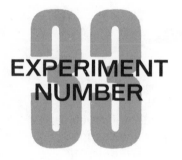

## EXPERIMENT NUMBER 33

**BACKGROUND:** This meditation, repeating the theme both of number 26 and number 39, is modeled on the popular programs of the same name. The topic, probably the most important of all we tackle in these prayer experiments, bears repeating in as many ways as we can devise.

**MATERIALS:** Optional, but very helpful: "Judgment Day" music, preferably the opening two and a half minutes of Richard Strauss' *Thus Spake Zarathustra* (more recently used to open the film *2001, A Space Odyssey*). If this music is not available, substitute something that sounds "judgmental." Candles are very good for this experiment.

**CURRICULUM TIE-IN:** Judgment Day, death, eternity; purpose of life; vocation, the future.

**PREPARATION OF CLASS:** Usual. Also, you might explain that the purpose of this experiment is to help us get some perspective on our lives, because we're usually so close to ourselves that we don't stand back and see our life span as a total unit, in need of tender, loving care.

---

"Now, get comfortable and still, and then please close your eyes so you can imagine things better. At the end of this meditation there will be some music. . . . The rest will all be in your head. . . .

*(if there really will be)*

"It's 19.... now. Let's begin to go back in time. Would you please try to imagine how you felt at the following times . . . last summer: What was the best thing you did? . . . And when you entered junior high school, how did you feel? Was it big? Strange? . . .

*(Adjust to suit age of students.)*

"And let's go back to fourth grade. . . . Do you remember your teacher? What was her name? What did she look like? . . .

"And now you're about seven or eight, and it's your First Communion day. . . . Are you concentrating on what it's all about? or looking at the other kids and their clothes? . . .

"And let's go back to your first day of school. . . . Do you remember how you felt? Happy? Afraid? . . .

"Now, we're going way back to when you first began to walk. . . . You were probably about one year old, and maybe you've seen pictures of yourself at this age. . . . Can you imagine yourself taking your first steps? . . .

"We're back to the day you were born. There you are in the hospital in the little buggy, like a supermarket basket, in a pink or a blue blanket. . . .

"We're come to the beginning of your life. Let's move up to the present; you're two, four, six, eight, ten, and it's today . . . and we're going on to the future. . . .

*(Count by twos to about where students are at present.)*

*(Adjust to fit class.)*

"You're a little older, and starting high school. . . . Which one will you be going to? . . . It's bigger; what will it be like? . . . How will you feel? . . .

"You're graduating from high school (no dropping out). . . . Your family is proud of you. . . .

(Be careful if you have even one student whose family couldn't care less.)

"And you have your first full-time job that summer, and are getting your first pay check. . . . What will you buy with it? . . .

"For the sake of uniformity, although this may not fit everyone's life, let's assume that you won't be single. . . . Can you picture 'Mr. Right,' girls? Boys, dream up some lovely bride for yourselves. . . .

"And now we're at your wedding. Is it a big church wedding, or are you eloping to save a lot of fuss and money? . . .

"Quickly we're jumping ahead to the day when you hold your first baby in your arms. This is such a special day. . . . Let's assume it's a little girl. . . .

"And now it's your 40th birthday, and your little girl is going on her first date. Mothers, you feel a little weepy. . . . fathers, you're trying to size up the guy. . . . Will he take good care of your 'little girl' or is he a bum? . . .

"Racing on, you're at the same daughter's graduation from high school. . . . You're getting very grey now. Mothers, you're using something to cover it up. . . .

"You're 55. . . . No use trying to cover the grey any longer. . . .

"You have a heart attack. . . . There's no hope. . . .

"You're dead . . . there you are, laid out in your coffin, with the family gathered around. . . . Is there a wake? Then there's the funeral. . . . Are there lots of flowers? Music? Where is the cemetery? Can you see the tombstone, with your name and 'Born 19....,' 'Died 20....'? . . .

*(As in so many aspects of teaching, you must know your class; if someone has lost a parent or close family member you may want to soft-pedal this part, or perhaps not use this experiment at all; or save it for a day when a vulnerable student is out.)*

"And that's the end of your body . . . but not of you. . . .

"When your body died, your soul left it and went somewhere to meet God. . . . Where do you picture him? On a throne? In a field? Downtown? . . . What's it like being with him? . . .

"And God is saying to you, 'Well, ........................ (fill in your name), I gave you x number of years. . . . Tell me, what did you do with them?' . . .

"You have to give God some sort of answer. What are you going to say to him? . . . try to imagine your answer, and yourself giving the answer, while this music plays. . . .

(If no music, you can say "while we are quiet for a minute.")

"Now, coming back slowly to the classroom and to 19...., we might think about whether or not we were satisfied with our answers. Of course, none of us knows what we will say to God on that day, but someday each of us will have to say something. . . ."

**DATE TRIED:**                    **TIME:**                    **REPEAT?:**

**RESULTS:**

# The Garden Meditation

**EXPERIMENT NUMBER 34**

**BACKGROUND:** This and the TV Meditation (No. 37) both have the theme of self-improvement, reinforcing each other. The "enclosed garden" theme is as old as the *Song of Solomon,* and is symbolic of paradise.

**MATERIALS:** None, although candles help. Plants for atmosphere?

**CURRICULUM TIE-IN:** Virtues, human potential; grace; symbols and signs.

**PREPARATION OF CLASS:** Usual.

"We're going to try another yoga-type meditation today, so I'll ask you to get as comfortable as you can; relax; close your eyes and see if you'd like to follow along as I suggest a few things to you.

"Can you, in your mind, create a beautiful garden? It can be any sort you like: an old-fashioned garden with flowers, or a tropical spot with exotic plants, or maybe a woodland garden that's all green and ferny. . . .

"Next, put some sort of boundary around it—a wall or a fence or a stream. . . .

"Imagine that this garden represents you, just as you are now. Think of the beautiful things growing in it—flowers, bushes, trees. . . . These are symbols of all the many good things about you, all the nice qualities you have. . . .

"In the garden, however, there are a few weeds growing. And these stand for, as you've probably guessed, the qualities you're not so happy to have, the things about yourself you'd like to get rid of. . . .

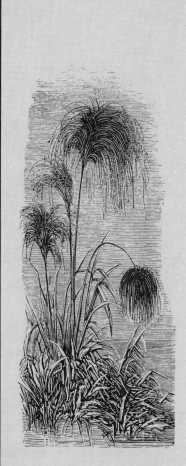

"Can you picture a few weeds? . . . They grow fast, and they wrap themselves around all the other plants, choking them, smothering them, using up all the energy in the garden. . . .

"Now, can you get rid of the weeds? Pull them up, or dig them out . . . somehow, see them wither and die. . . .

"Almost without your noticing it, a gentle rain has begun to fall and water the garden. You can probably guess what the rain symbolizes. . . . It's God's grace, and it will help all the good things in you to grow. . . .

"Finally, while we're quietly relaxing here, let's each take time to ask for God's help as the virtues and good things in us grow, all through our lives. . . .

*(Or, if you've had a good bit of "prayer to ourselves" lately, you might want to make up a prayer at this point.)*

"We'll leave our gardens now, and come back to the classroom. Let's remember though, that we're 'becoming' all the time. . . . How many people felt this meditation worked for them? . . ."

*(Why or why not?)*

**DATE TRIED:**  **TIME:**  **REPEAT?:**

**RESULTS:**

# Floating on a Cloud Meditation

## EXPERIMENT NUMBER 35

**BACKGROUND:** This is the most "physical" and far out of any of the prayer experiments. Ideally, it is best experienced lying on the floor, but this may seem too risky to many teachers (and students), suggesting a lack of classroom decorum. Consider tossing out decorum just this once, checking with your principal first to avoid shocking him (and being fired yourself).

**MATERIALS:** None. Some way of dimming the lighting, by candles or other means, would be very helpful.

**CURRICULUM TIE-IN:** Presence of God; materialism.

**PREPARATION OF CLASS:** Usual, plus a special urging to try wholeheartedly to enter into the spirit of this rather unusual meditation.

---

"This is a very Indian sort of meditation we're going to try today. See if you can let it work for you. First, you must get very, very comfortable. . . .

*(on the floor?—how clean is yours?)*

"Now see, first, if you can relax every muscle in your body. Let yourself go limp. Breathe slowly. Try to be serious, because the experiment won't work well if you aren't. People all over the world do things like this every day, so we're not really so strange as you may think. . . .

*(Speak softly and slowly, in cloud fashion.)*

Next, pretend—and this is possible only if you concentrate—that your body is being lifted on a soft, fluffy (but strong) cloud. . . . First, it's just being lifted a little, then up to the ceiling. Finally, the cloud is taking you through the roof, out into the air. The roof just melted away. . . . It's summer, so you don't have to worry about leaving your coat behind. How does it feel? . . .

*(Prediction: One out of a thousand students will be able to do this seriously. That's O.K. You're exposing them to something of value, even if they don't get it completely now.)*

142

"Now the cloud starts moving horizontally. You're above the earth, as if in a plane. You've started circling the globe, like an astronaut, but much more slowly. Can you see houses? . . . Cars? . . . Fields in patterns like a quilt? . . . Rivers winding like snakes? . . . Think of the earth, its continents, the oceans. . . . Think of the pictures of earth men in space have taken. . . .

"And, most important of all, because you're not tied to the earth by gravity anymore, you are very aware of the presence of God all around you. Of course, you knew he was back on earth when you were there, but things often got in the way of your awareness of him. Up here there's nothing to interfere. See if you can sense his presence. . . . Can you make any sort of connection with him, communicate with him at all? . . . Perhaps just rest in him?

*(Allow a minute or so.)*

"Each one of us is going to return to earth now, slowly . . . your cloud is settling over this building, I hope. Don't try to make it come down over the movie theatre or the Dairy Queen. . . . You're over our roof, hovering like a helicopter or a humming bird . . . and you're coming through it . . . and you're back where you started, landing very gently. . . .

*(Use your local spots.)*

*(someone's sure to crash-land)*

"And here we are back in the classroom again. You can open your eyes now. Did we lose anyone? . . . I wonder if any of you feel as if you've brought God back with you, just a little. . . .

"This trip improves greatly with practice, so if you liked this experiment perhaps you'll try it again at home and see what happens. Would anyone like to share any of his feelings with us? . . ."

*(If there's time you might want to ask if anyone remembers a time when Jesus was able to pass through solid walls. See Jn 20:19: after the Resurrection.)*

**DATE TRIED:**                    **TIME:**                    **REPEAT?:**

**RESULTS:**

# Escape Meditation

**EXPERIMENT NUMBER 36**

**BACKGROUND:** Yogis (those who practice yoga) call this the "creation of a mental ashram (hermitage)." Teachers may find they need to get away from it all a lot more than do their students!

**MATERIALS:** None. Candles in the dark are nice.

**CURRICULUM TIE-IN:** Presence of God; retreat, peace.

**PREPARATION OF CLASS:** Usual.

"Please settle down, get comfortable and close your eyes. Would you think, of all the places there are in the world, which is your favorite? . . . the beach? a big city? a mountaintop? a small town like this one? a farm? on the ocean? up in the sky? an island? a hidden valley? a jungle rain forest?

"And would you think now, at which time of the year is this place you have chosen best? . . . If you picked a farm in the country, is it nicest in the spring at planting time, or when the leaves have turned in the fall? . . .

"And now, if you could choose any sort of house in which to live, and have it on the place you've chosen, what kind of dwelling would you have? . . . a tree house? a colonial farmhouse? a penthouse on top of a tall apartment in the city? a castle? a teepee? a dome? if on the ocean, a yacht? or a Chinese houseboat? if in the sky, a luxury airplane? . . .

*(Adjust to suit your circumstances.)*

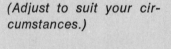

145

"And what view would you have from the windows of your house, or whatever you've chosen? . . . If at the beach, waves? or sand dunes? a garden? mountains? sky? a waterfall?

(Expect snickers from boys 12 and over: "No, John, you're all alone.")

"Going inside your home now, let's pretend that inside this dwelling you have a room all your own. It's absolutely private. No one else can ever go in. How would you furnish it? What would be in it? . . .

"Would you have comfortable furniture? a stereo and a good record collection? posters? a refrigerator for goodies? books? a TV set? indoor pool? ten years' back issues of *Mad*? . . . What colors would the room be? . . .

"Now this room, in this house, in this spot, is all yours. It's a place of perfect peace and quiet, much more so than any place you could find here in *(your city)*. It's a place where you enjoy yourself and have fun, and where you can relax, and also where—because it is so peaceful—you feel very close to God. You seem to find him here whenever you go into your 'escape room,' and you get in the habit of feeling that he's there with you, that you're not alone.

"Pretend you're there now and see if you can find him there too. You don't have to talk to him; just be aware of his presence. . . .

146

"Now we're going to come back to the classroom, but remember that you have this place of your own in your mind, and you can go back to it any time at all. You can find peace there and find God there. Keep it just for yourself. Many of the saints did this; St. Catherine of Siena called her place her 'inner cell.' As you know, God is always with us, in the people and places around us and inside us, just like a fish is in water and water is in the fish (St. Catherine said that too). What we have done in this experiment is create a special sort of place to find God in our imagination; sometimes when the ordinary ways don't work so well, retreating to our own special 'escape' spot helps."

**DATE TRIED:**                **TIME:**                **REPEAT?:**

**RESULTS:**

## TV Meditation

**EXPERIMENT NUMBER 87**

**BACKGROUND:** This experiment is a complement to the Garden Meditation (No. 34), stressing growth in virtue through grace.

**MATERIALS:** None. Candles, as usual, add a touch.

**CURRICULUM TIE-IN:** Virtues, human potential; grace.

**PREPARATION OF CLASS:** Usual.

"Will you get settled for this meditation, please? Try to close your eyes and relax. Now, see if you can visualize, on the inside of your eyelids, a solid color screen, like a TV screen. This isn't easy to do the first time, but give it a try. . . .

"And now, try to project on the screen a picture of yourself doing something you consider to be your worst fault. For example, do you fight with your younger brother or sister? . . . or an older one? . . . Try to picture the two of you arguing. . . .

"Or, perhaps you feel you're not always a very good sport. Can you picture yourself having something crummy to say to someone on your team when you've lost a close game? . . .

"And now, remembering that God is always with us, in each of our souls, let's tune him in for a minute and tell him that we think our worst fault is ................................., and that we'd like his help in being the opposite. . . . We'll take half a minute for this prayer. . . .

*(Choose examples suitable to your class.)*

148

"Is your TV screen still there? . . . Here's the hard part. Can you picture yourself, acting as you were before, being wrapped with God's grace? . . . It can take any form you like: a gentle breath, or a stiff breeze, if you like the wind idea; or it might be like rain falling on you (as in the Garden Meditation). . . . Or you might not want to give it any form at all, but just be aware that he's sending his grace to you. . . .

*(if you did that experiment)*

"Finally, on your TV screen, picture the original situation again . . . but this time filled with the grace God has sent you. You've changed! How are you acting now? . . . When little Joey messes up your history project, you're being patient with him, aren't you? (Well, more patient than before, at any rate.) . . . Or were you originally giving your mother some flak about taking out the garbage? . . . See how graciously you're helping her now? You *are* helping her, aren't you? . . .

*(Allow for some vocal reactions here.)*

"Well, this TV show is over, but I'd like to suggest that you rerun it before long. See if you can get very good at imagining yourself on your own interior screen; work on different faults; see if it seems to help. . . . Would anyone be willing to share his 'show' with us? . . ."

**DATE TRIED:**          **TIME:**                    **REPEAT?:**

**RESULTS:**

# Valentine Meditation

**EXPERIMENT NUMBER 38**

**MATERIALS:** None necessary, but candles help and you might want to decorate with hearts.

**CURRICULUM TIE-IN:** Valentine's Day, St. Valentine, love; thanksgiving.

**PREPARATION OF CLASS:** Usual, plus any profound or not-so-profound thoughts on love you may want to add, especially on the misuse of that word.

---

"Today we'll try another of the yoga-type meditations. Remember, if you don't go for these you're perfectly free to tune out for a few minutes. This is an easy one. Will you get comfortable now? . . . Really relax, close your eyes and try to put everything else out of your mind for a short time. . . .

"This is called the Valentine Meditation, because it's about love. We each have had some love in our life, but it's possible that we take it for granted. The idea of this meditation is to help us appreciate the love we have had.

"First, we'll start with something simple. Have you ever loved a place? . . . If you have, see if you can picture it in your imagination. Maybe it's your room, or your home, or your grandparents' home, or a church, or some outdoor spot, or even someplace you read about or made up or saw in a movie and have never even visited. . . . Can you see it in your mind? . . .

*(Allow time.)*

150

"Next, were you ever lucky enough to have an animal love you? . . . maybe a dog?  Can you picture his wet nose? . . . his chops? . . . or a cat?  Can you see its beautiful yellow—or are they green—eyes? . . . its graceful walk? . . . any other animals? . . .

*(If your students live on farms, adjust your examples.)*

"And finally, people.  Who has loved you? . . . and who are the ones you've loved? . . . Can you picture each one of them in your mind now? . . . family members, relatives, friends, old people, very young children, a teacher, someone from church. . . .

*(Avoid, again, saying "your father," "your mother"; many students would be quick to say their parents don't love them. And occasionally it may even be true. )*

"Now, if you'd like to, why not take this time to thank God for the love you've known in your lifetime?  There might be a lot you could say to him about love in the past, present and future. . . .

*(Allow about 60 seconds.)*

"We have to come back to the religion classroom now.  I'm sure this was one place all of you included under your 'places I've loved' heading, wasn't it? . . ."

*(to be said with appropriately naive expression)*

**DATE TRIED:**          **TIME:**          **REPEAT?:**

**RESULTS:**

151

# chapter 8
# PRAYERS NEEDING PROPS

Some of the props for the prayer experiments described in this chapter are simple: pictures, plants, a folding screen. Some are the usual audiovisual tools, here pressed into service as prayer-starters: a tape recorder, slides, films, the opaque projector.

Believe it, there's bound to be a day when you're lugging a 25-pound screen through a downpour and will ask yourself, "Is it worth all the hassle?" (Author's best memory along these lines: armed with huge posters and a tangling mobile, snow and night whirling all around, meeting another eighth-grade teacher. He is toting—for Hanukkah celebration re Jesus' boyhood—one box of dradles borrowed from rabbi, big pan of potato pancakes his wife made, plus portable oven to heat them. Other teacher: "What in hell are we dragging all this stuff around for?") You'll know as you ask, as we did, that if it helps even one or two of your students find another way to reach God, it's worth it. Neither rain nor snow. . . .

The audiovisual machines are familiar to most teachers and, if not, you can always find someone to help you break in to them. Of course, in using any equipment you will want to be at ease with it before trying it out in class. The teacher whose teeth are gritted as if he were going into surgery—because he's not comfortable with some mechanical device—is asking his students to tune out. We need enough familiarity with machines so we won't come unglued if they balk on us.

Slides deserve a few lines of their own; they are an especially valuable tool, both because of their versatility and because you can talk and discuss while using them (as you cannot with a sound filmstrip). There are fine sets of slides for religious education to be purchased, and most have excellent guidelines for their use in their folders or notebooks. You can also photograph your own slides or make (with pressure-sensitive adhesive) homemade "lift slides."

Slides, however, seem to be an easy medium to misuse. They are often shown just because they are available, without great concern for a good fit between slide and subject. For example, to the words of a song someone will flash slides chosen from what he had access to, but not really having any great connection with the song or any great relevance to the students. Result: boredom, confusion and time wasted because medium and idea were not dovetailed. Yet these same slides used accurately at the right time are a superb learning tool. We should also remember that a distinctive slide can be used effectively only once with a class.

153

With slides we have to beware of giving the students too much to grasp at one time. For instance, a slide show plus readings plus music can be a lot to handle mentally at first hearing, a sensory overload. The teacher more or less loses his perspective while putting something like this together, forgetting what its *initial* impact will be. Keep it simple, fluid, clear.

A common slide failure is to project shots too slowly. If your pace winds down, so will the pace of your students' minds. This, plus the darkened room, is conducive to one thing—sleep.

Several of the prayer experiments before this can be worked out with slides (see Experiment No. 28, Castle Meditation, and No. 31, Heaven Meditation, among others) *if* you can get your hands on good slides. If not, forget it.

There is one aspect of audiovisual presentations that's of special interest in relation to prayer experiments. That is the darkened, preferably blackened, room. Apart from our concern that some student may see the cover of darkness as a golden chance to disappear, the lights-out situation can lead to a couple of other problems.

One is the temptation (from which adults are not free either) to start talking during the blackout. Usually a reminder about behavior standards *before* darkening the room is sufficient; however, if the noise level is unacceptable to you, the teacher, (and, in the case of prayer, this means any noise at all) don't hesitate to stop and turn on the lights or draw open the curtains. This is better than trying to pray over an undercurrent of buzzing. A second chance will usually be appreciated.

The other potential problem is that lights-out time may turn into make-out time, at least with ninth-graders and older students. (The author writes from New England; maybe where you are it would be sixth-graders and up, God forbid!) Now, while it's true that love is the great theme of all religion classes, still we have to make it clear to an amorous-looking group that we're conducting experiments in *prayer,* not in anything else. And make it clear before the lights go out!

# "This Is Your Life" in Slides

**EXPERIMENT NUMBER 38**

**BACKGROUND:** A third round of this vital theme, repeating the sentiments of Experiments No. 26 and No. 33.

**MATERIALS:** Slide projector and screen or wall; slides (no more than 50) covering a life span, from infancy to old age, in order. Include pictures of both sexes.

**CURRICULUM TIE-IN:** Purpose of life; death, eternity; vocation, the future.

**PREPARATION OF CLASS:** Usual, plus any words of wisdom necessary on behavior in a dark room. Invite comments as you go.

---

"This slide show is going to be about a life; it will be about your life. If some of the details are different, just overlook that.

"You're born . . . here you are as a baby. . . .

*(Fit your commentary to whatever slides you've come up with; talk it just as though to a home audience.)*

"And here you are about the time you started school. Think how much lies ahead of you. . . .

*(If you take your own slides, shots of your town —even of your students —will make this even more effective.)*

"And here you are now. What sort of dreams do you have for the future? . . .

*(pictures of kids the age of your students)*

"What's ahead? We can only guess, but let's do that. Some young people, we know, go downhill quickly and even throw their lives away. . . .

(Some of the purchased sets of slides have drug-abuse pictures.)

"We won't plan on that for you, certainly. Let's assume that you get involved in some sort of interesting work once you've finished school. . . . Girls, will you be career women? . . . or will you join one of the women's services? . . . Boys, will you, perhaps, be coaching younger boys in sports? . . . or do you think you'll enlist? . . .

*(Adjust to fit the slides you have.)*

"You may decide to marry, if the right person comes along. . . .

"Or you may not. . . .

"Let's see how you look at about 50. What sort of life have you led? Have you done the things you had dreamed of when you were younger? . . .

*(As all through this experiment, slides should be of both males and females.)*

"And, perhaps, you'll live to be an old person, someone about 75 or 80. How do you think you'll feel inside when you're looking like this? old? or young? . . . Will you still have dreams of things to accomplish? Will you be ready to die? . . .

*(Let students fill in details.)*

"Someday, for everyone, the 'x' number of years God's given him will be up. Maybe it will happen when you're elderly, maybe when you're much younger. But the day will come. . . .

*(If you have no suitable death slide, tape an opaque piece of paper to another slide to black out all light.)*

"Here in the dark, thinking about each of our life spans, is there anyone who would be willing to make up some sort of prayer for us, a prayer based on the look at life we've just tried to take? . . .

*(If not, have a quickie ready yourself.)*

"Let's come 'back to life' now. Could I suggest that this is a good topic to give thought to from time to time? Not that dwelling on death is the point, because it isn't, but that one can't really live well until he's accepted the fact of his death—someday."

**DATE TRIED:**          **TIME:**          **REPEAT?:**

**RESULTS:**

# Plant Prayer

**EXPERIMENT NUMBER 40**

**BACKGROUND:** This experiment is based on the studies which have shown the power of prayer to grow plants. It is a good project to span several months, even a school year, being repeated every month, or even every week.

**MATERIALS:** Two identical plants in pots marked "A" and "B" (or something else); you might sprout beans yourself. Before class, measure plants, and arrange some plan for caring for them in the classroom (carrying them home and back might disturb the experiment).

**CURRICULUM TIE-IN:** Prayer power; faith; unity of all living things, creation.

**PREPARATION OF CLASS:** Usual.

---

"Today we have a very interesting experiment that will take a little time to explain. Perhaps you've read of the different experiments proving that plants seem to have 'feelings'—for example, the work of Cleve Backster and his lie detector. There have also been experiments showing that plants respond to the power of prayer!

*(If you know about this, or students do, elaborate. Do you talk to your plants? play music for them?)*

"The Rev. Franklin Loehr, a minister, has conducted over 900 experiments in plant-praying and has proved that it works. The plants prayed for grow taller and healthier. I thought you might like to try it here. . . .

*(His book is* The Power of Prayer on Plants, *published by Doubleday in 1959.)*

"Here we have two *(variety)* plants, both ............ inches tall. Would someone like to be our recorder to measure each time we pray, and keep a record of whether or not our experiment works? . . .

*(Try to pick someone who never gets to do much else.)*

"One Sunday morning in church, the Reverend Loehr asked his congregation to direct intensive prayers toward one of the two plants he showed them. That's what we'll try to do, and we'll see if our prayers help one of our plants to grow. Which one shall we pray for? . . .

*(Vote.)*

"Now, if you want to participate in this experiment, let's take 15 seconds and ask God silently to help plant *(A or B)* to grow strong and tall and straight. Remember, this is not a stunt, but can help us see something very basic about God. What can it show us? . . .

*(The answer you're fishing for is "God answers prayers" or "prayer works.")*

"When I say 'Go,' let's each pray in our own way for plant ..............  Go . . .

"Fine. Now during the week these two plants will have exactly the same care. They'll both have the same amount of light and water, which will be measured. Then in a week we'll see if plant ........ has grown any more than plant .............  One week from today, our recorder will measure the two plants before class and see what has happened. . . .

*(Tell class your plans for caring for plants.)*

*(Measure in a week; if no change, maybe you need more and better praying. If the neglected plant grows more, keep trying or suspect sabotage!)*

"Do you think it will work? . . . or do you think I've gone a little batty? (don't answer that). . . ."

**DATE TRIED:**          **TIME:**          **REPEAT?:**

**RESULTS:**

# Closeness Prayer

## EXPERIMENT NUMBER 41

**BACKGROUND:** This prayer experiment takes more time than most and requires an opaque projector, although you can translate it into an art or drawing experiment if done without a projector. Something about sharing experiences in the dark, through the medium of sketches, seems to make students more vocal than usual and makes the extra fuss and time a good investment.

**MATERIALS:** Opaque projector and screen; pencils and *white* paper cut to fit the size of the projector.

**CURRICULUM TIE-IN:** Spiritual life, presence of God.

**PREPARATION OF CLASS:** Usual. Give out pencils and paper, reassuring class that this is not an art contest.

---

"Today for our prayer experiment we're going to try something very special. Each of us has had at least one experience we can share with the rest of the class which will help them grow. Now, we don't have to share this experience, but maybe it's sort of selfish not to. So, if you're willing, let's try this.

"First, let's stop, collect ourselves, and ask God to do something for us. We surely have each had times in our lives when we've felt especially close to him; perhaps just a moment, or perhaps for a longer stretch of time. Would you ask him now—as I will—to help you remember one of those times? . . .

"And now, on your paper, could you draw—just in stick figures, if you like, or even in symbols—that time? . . . Where were you? . . . Who was with you? . . . What were you doing? . . . See if you can just get the general setting of this time you felt close to God down on your paper. . . . Make your lines on the heavy side. . . .

*(Avoid giving specific suggestions of when anyone might have felt close to God.)*

*(You do it too, and make sure your art work isn't too professional.)*

"Good. Now, I'm going to ask you if you'll be willing to share your experience with the rest of the class. How can this help anyone else? . . .

"I have an opaque projector here, and each one who is willing can have his sketch projected on the screen, while he describes the time he chose. . . . I'll start with mine. . . .

*(If no projector, drawings on art paper can be held up close to students.)*

"Is there anyone else who's willing to share his 'time of closeness' with us? . . .

*(You won't insist, of course, but you might ask specific students if they wouldn't like to "exhibit"; once someone breaks the ice most will want to see how their drawing projects.)*

"Thank you. That was good!"

*(It's almost sure to have been good.)*

*(Collect pencils.)*

**DATE TRIED:**            **TIME:**            **REPEAT?:**

**RESULTS:**

# The Isolation Prayer

**EXPERIMENT NUMBER 42**

**MATERIALS:** Folding screen; at least one movable chair. Prayer book, or a few prayers you or students have written.

**CURRICULUM TIE-IN:** Prayer.

**PREPARATION OF CLASS:** Usual. Arrange desks (if movable) on one side of room. As far away as possible, stand screen around another desk or chair, leaving an opening large enough for someone to enter the cubbyhole. The opening should face away from the rest of the class. If without a screen, you could rig up a curtain on a string at one corner of the room.

"We've talked about how we pray, and with whom we pray, and what we pray about, and when we pray, and why we pray. Today we have an experiment which will help us see if it makes any difference *where* we pray. You can see that we have one chair isolated from the rest of the class. Jesus said, '. . . when you pray, enter into your closet, and when you have shut your door, pray to your Father . . . in secret. . . .' What do you think he meant? . . . Shall we put someone in the closet to help him pray? . . .

*(Mt 6:6)*

*(Hopefully someone will come up with the idea of solitude.)*

"Group prayer or shared prayer is very wonderful, especially once you get over the strangeness of it, but it's not the only sort of prayer, as you know. There are times when we have to be alone with God, and many feel that one of the great failings of our century is that people don't arrange to be alone with God regularly. . . .

"Now, of course, we can't experiment too much with being alone when there are ........... of us here. But we can try something that might help convince us of the need to be alone with God more often. Here we have an 'isolation booth,' not quite as fancy as the ones on TV shows. We're going to read a few prayers, and for each one I'll ask for a volunteer to enter the isolation booth. The person inside the booth has to attempt to judge whether it's any easier for him to pray apart from us than with us. Who would like to be first? . . .

(a good chance to pick someone who rarely participates)

"Thank you, ....................... Now go behind the screen, and sit down comfortably. Let's get in the right frame of mind for praying, and read this prayer. Please remember that listening to someone read isn't the same as praying; we each have to try to make the prayer our own, inside. ................., behind the screen, see if you can do the same. Who'd like to read this prayer? . . .

(Anything will do; do you have some prayers left from Experiment No. 6?)

"Now we'll switch people. ............, will you come out from behind the screen, and will someone else take his place? . . .

"Thank you, ................. ............, you sit with the class now, and we'll repeat the experiment with a similar prayer. .............., behind the screen, see if you can make this your own prayer. Who'd like to read the second prayer? . . .

(It should be similar to the first, for control purposes.)

"Good. Now, ................, if you'll come out we'll ask both of our experimenters to tell us if being away from the group makes any difference in praying. . . .

(If they just say yes—or no—try to dig for specifics; what was the difference, if any? Why do they think this occurred? etc.)

"Would anyone else like to try it now? . . .

(Have extra prayers ready for another round or two.)

"I'll leave the screen in class. Each time we have a prayer experiment, someone can try it from inside the isolation booth. Obviously, the situation here is rigged, but the important question is, 'What carry-over can this experiment have to my everyday life?' . . .

*(an interesting point to discuss)*

*(This can be tacked on, but only with a class which permits you an occasional homily; not all classes bear up gracefully!)*

"Many young people, as they grow older, give up prayer on their own. They think of 'saying their prayers' as a childish habit they've outgrown. Then, when they go to church, they find they get very little out of it because they've brought very little with them. This way their whole relationship with God can crumble. Maybe the Isolation Prayer will remind each of us how much we need to make time, regularly, to be alone with God."

**DATE TRIED:**        **TIME:**        **REPEAT?:**

**RESULTS:**

# The Tape-Recorder Prayer

## EXPERIMENT NUMBER 43

**BACKGROUND:** Do this only if you have a student you can trust with a tape recorder outside of class, either yours or his.

**MATERIALS:** Tape recorder. Five to ten minutes of taped interviews, gathered by one student (or a team of students). Half a dozen Christians, representing a cross section of ages and occupations, should be asked how they feel about Jesus of Nazareth, or some other thoughtful question. Each speaker should be identified by the interviewer, not by name, but by sex, approximate age and occupation.

**CURRICULUM TIE-IN:** Maturity in faith; witness.

**PREPARATION OF CLASS:** Usual.

---

"Today we have a very interesting tape that ................ has made for us on his own time. He has interviewed some people about their religion and taped their answers. ................, would you like to tell the class what you asked these people and something about their reactions in general? . . .

"Let's listen to the tape now. . . .

*(Interviewer may want to stop before each person on tape and describe.)*

"We've heard people telling how they feel about their religion on this tape. I wonder now if you would stop, and talk to God in your own soul about this same question. . . . How do *you* feel about Jesus of Nazareth? . . .

*(or whatever the question was; this could lead to written interviews by other class members.)*

"You may have discovered you don't have a very definite reaction to this question; maybe you don't know how to answer it. If that's so, it's worth thinking over—and praying over—on your own."

**DATE TRIED:**                    **TIME:**                    **REPEAT?:**

**RESULTS:**

# Pictures' Prayer

## EXPERIMENT NUMBER 44

**MATERIALS:** Photographs (from magazines) of real people, everyday people, one for each student. Aim for a cross section of the human race; avoid public figures, ridiculous pictures and models whose faces are extremely familiar, like Josephine the Plumber and Betty Crocker.

**CURRICULUM TIE-IN:** People, brotherhood.

**PREPARATION OF CLASS:** Usual.

---

"I'm going to give everyone a picture of someone, another human being. Look at the person you get carefully. . . .

"How about making up some details about your person? Can you give him or her a name—nothing silly, but a name that really seems to fit the face? . . .

"Decide how old he or she is . . . where he lives . . . what he does with his time . . . what his life style is. . . .

"Now, most important, what do you think are the difficulties of your person's life? If you have, for example, an elderly person, what problems do you think his age brings? . . . Or is your person black? . . . What problems might he have because of his race? . . . If your person's a parent, what do you think he loses sleep over? . . .

*(if possible, pictures of girls and women to the girls, boys and men to your boys)*

"Who would like to show us his person and tell us what he's like? . . .

(As many as time allows, or you could pair up students and let each tell his partner.)

"Finally, let's imagine that each of our people is a symbol of all the other people in the world who are like him or her. For example, if you have a boy about 16, with a home problem, let's say that he stands for all boys in their midteens with problems at home.

"Can you take about 30 seconds now to ask God's help for all the people symbolized by your person? . . .

*(Remember, it takes many tries for these silent moments to become comfortable and then fruitful; don't get discouraged.)*

"Would anyone be willing to share his prayer with all of us? . . . Do you ever pray for people you don't know? . . ."

*(For example, those whose nations are at war, the sick, the dying, accident victims, and so on. You might make a list of these categories of "nameless people" on the board.)*

**DATE TRIED:**　　　　　　　**TIME:**　　　　　　　**REPEAT?:**

**RESULTS:**

# The Rebus Prayer

## EXPERIMENT NUMBER 45

**MATERIALS:** The "prop" here is your rebus puzzle and some faint ability to sketch it on the board. The rebus below is the opening of Psalm 41, a wonderful prayer: "As the deer longs for running water, so my soul longs for you, Oh God. . . ." You can make up your own. Remember, artistic ability is not the point; your students will have great fun razzing you about the ass that looks like a dog (as does the one below). Colored chalks are useful, but not essential.

**CURRICULUM TIE-IN:** Depends on prayer chosen. In this case, the tie-in would be the spiritual life.

**PREPARATION OF CLASS:** Usual.

"This is a rebus, a puzzle where symbols and pictures stand for words and syllables. This one is also a prayer, one of the psalms in fact, and I wonder if you can translate it together so we can pray it. . . .

*(Work through the rebus, giving generous clues, and putting correct words under pictures on board.)*

*As the deer*

*longs for running*

*water, sew (so)*

169

m eye (my) s owl (soul)

l ong s (longs) for

(or if you can do it, try King Kong, minus a crowned head, minus K.)

you, Oh

G od (God)

("How are we supposed to know it's a codfish?" Answer: "You're just supposed to.")

(Pray the psalm verse once everyone is ready.)

"Very good! Now, let's pray the prayer we've unscrambled. Would someone like to do it for us, or shall we all do it together? . . . First, let's pull ourselves together and get in the right frame of mind for praying. . . .

"Why don't you see if you can make up a prayer like this for the rest of the class to work out?"

**DATE TRIED:**                    **TIME:**                    **REPEAT?:**

**RESULTS:**

# A Superprayer Experiment

**EXPERIMENT NUMBER 40**

**BACKGROUND:** If you've had good luck with prayer experiments and your class, you might want to try this one- or two-hour-long prayer experiment—or you might describe it briefly ahead of time and let your students vote on whether or not to tackle it. In three parts, it combines most of the techniques used in earlier experiments, and has several moments of prayer.

Part I, the musical section, takes almost an entire class; the music alone plays for a half hour. Part I can stand by itself, or be followed up at the next class by either Part II or Part III, or both. Why not see how Part I goes before deciding what comes next—if anything?

You will recognize the multiple-doors image from many children's stories: *Alice in Wonderland,* Maeterlinck's *The Blue-bird,* and even *Bluebeard.*

**MATERIALS:** Record or tape of Moussorgsky's *Pictures at an Exhibition* (as always, however, you may have to adapt ideas to fit whatever music is available). The notes given here are for the orchestral version, which is a little easier for students to follow than the original piano version. Be sure to listen to the music and think this experiment through before trying it in class; you'll want to get its divisions clear in your head.

Pencils and two pieces of paper for all.

Thirteen signs lettered (large enough for farthest student to read) as follows: WALK, No. 1-STATUS AND POSITION, No. 2-ROMANTIC LOVE, No. 3-LOVE OF NATURE, No. 4-FAME, No. 5-FAMILY LIFE, No. 6-MONEY, No. 7-FUN AND PLEASURE, No. 8-KNOWLEDGE, No. 9-SERVICE TO OTHERS, No. 10-POWER, No. 11-GOD, and PRAY. (These words could be written on the board as needed instead of on signs.) Keep signs face down until used.

**CURRICULUM TIE-IN:** Philosophies of life; values, goals; witness.

**PREPARATION OF CLASS:** Usual. In addition, you might want to pay your class a deserved compliment by saying that only exceptional students could be asked to try this experiment.
Pass out pencils and paper.

# — PART I —

"We're going to try something special today, a very fancy prayer experiment. Would anyone like to launch us with a prayer that this helps some of us make contact with God? . . .

*(Guess who's ever ready and willing if no student offers!)*

"This prayer experiment has more than one part. The first part is a meditation to music, interrupted by thinking and writing, and it will take our entire class. The music we're going to use is called *Pictures at an Exhibition,* and it was written by a Russian composer, Moussorgsky, in 1893. Does anyone know the music? . . .

*(pronounced with accent on second syllable)*

"Moussorgsky opened his work with a musical theme representing himself as he walked around at an exhibit of a friend's paintings. Here's that theme. . . .

*(Play opening melody.)*

"He goes on to paint—in music—each of the pictures hanging on the walls, and between most of the pictures he goes back to his "walking theme," as though he were strolling through the art gallery.

"Now, because this music is so descriptive, it lends itself perfectly to a meditation for us. We're not going to an art gallery though. Here's what I'd like to ask you to try—it's harder than anything we've done before and will really be a test of how good you are as prayer experimenters.

"When the music starts, close your eyes and try to imagine yourself in a long, dark corridor or tunnel. You are walking (to the walking music) and you see that this hall you are in has 11

doors in it, each with a sign over it. When the music changes (originally, of course, to indicate the first picture at the exhibition) imagine that you have stopped before the first door. I'll hold up the sign that's supposedly over that door; open your eyes and look at it. Each of the 11 doors will have its own different sign.

"O.K. so far? . . . Now, each sign will tell you of some value around which people center their lives. We can have many values in our lives, of course, but everyone seems to have one love, one interest, which is central to all his decisions and behavior. Can you guess what some of these values might be? . . .

*(If not, you can mention a couple and perhaps illustrate with someone who lived by each philosophy—power, with Hitler as an example, and love of nature, with Thoreau and today's back-to-the-earth people for examples.)*

"There's one more thing. After you open your eyes and look at the sign which is supposed to be over each door, try to imagine yourself opening that door. What sort of room is inside? What might you find, for example, in a room with the word 'POWER' over the door? . . .

*(armies, bugging devices, a ranting demagogue, weapons, and dozens of other possibilities)*

"While the music for each room is playing, write down on your papers the number and title of the room, as on my sign, and then write down what you think you might find inside that room. It can have people in it, doing whatever you think they might do. It can have things in it, and be decorated any way you think is appropriate. Write down whatever you like.

"Then, when you hear the walking music again, close your eyes and pretend you're back in the corridor, moving along, until you hear a change in the music. This will mean you've reached the next room. Are you still with me? . . . Remember, try to describe each room on paper as we get to it.

"There's just a couple of fine points to cover, and then we'll start. There's no walking music before doors four, six, seven, eight and ten. We'll just go from one room to another on these.

"Also, when we get to door number 11, the last door, the 'walking music' will mix with the 'room music.' This means we should go into the room, and walk around it. Write what you might find there. Finally, when you hear music that sounds like gongs in this last room that'll be a signal for our prayer time— I'll hold up a sign that says 'PRAY' so you'll know where we are.

"Do anything you like. You might want to talk to God about your walk, or just be with him, or write a prayer, or do nothing at all. See what happens. The prayer time, which is also mixed with walking music, lasts about two minutes until the end of the piece.

"All set? . . . Once more, what do the signs over the doors stand for? . . .

*(philosophies of life, central values of life)*

*(Start music; hold up WALK sign; settle yourself somewhere where your signs can be seen, yet comfortably enough so you can listen and imagine and write along with your class.)*

"Here we go; get ready to descend into your tunnel. . . .

Here is a list of the order in which you will hold up your signs, or draw them on the board. You'll find they correlate with the music: WALK . . . No. 1-STATUS AND POSITION . . . WALK . . . No. 2-ROMANTIC LOVE . . . WALK . . . No. 3-LOVE OF NATURE . . . No. 4-FAME . . . WALK . . . No. 5-FAMILY LIFE . . . No. 6-MONEY . . . No. 7-FUN AND PLEASURE . . . No. 8-KNOWLEDGE . . . WALK . . . No. 9-SERVICE TO OTHERS (in the original music, numbers eight and nine are both included in one painting, "Catacombs," which has a walk in its middle) . . . No. 10-POWER . . . WALK . . . No. 11-GOD . . . PRAY.

"Well . . . what do you think? . . .

"We'll do something with your papers at our next class, so why don't you sign them and pass them over to the ends of each row. I promise not to look at them—it's just that you might forget to bring them back or your dogs might eat them.

*(Let everyone stretch, and see what sort of spontaneous reactions come out; if very cool, you'll probably want to forget about Parts II and III.)*

*(if you plan to go on)*

*(Collect pencils too.)*

## — PART II —

(Return papers; give out pencils.)

"At our last class, you'll remember (I hope) that we took a look at 11 different philosophies of life, 11 values which people have often made the central hinges of their lives, since history began. I'm going to divide you into ten groups and give each group one of the signs we used last time. You have your papers, and I'd like you to see if, in each group, you can agree on what the room you've been given was like. Who was in the room? . . . What was going on in there? . . . How was the room decorated and what was in it? . . . We'll save room 11 to discuss together.

*(if you had signs)*

*(Divide into groups of two or three, if enough students; if not, give some groups two rooms. Give out all signs except No. 11-GOD. Allow three minutes or so for discussion.)*

"Now, will each group in order come up and tell us what you decided? . . . and then, each of us, from our notes, can add any other bright ideas we may have had while listening to the music. Room number one? . . .

*(Group one, describing the room labeled STA-TUS AND POSITION, comes up; you may have to help with some leading questions.)*

"What do you all think, in general, of a life based on the search for status and position? . . . Is this a common philosophy of life today? . . . What would make someone decide on this as his way of life? . . . or do people actually sit down and make a decision to live as status seekers? Maybe they never think about it. . . . What do you think? . . .

*(These questions are for the entire class.)*

176

"Good, room one. Now room two. . . .

"Finally, we're up to room 11, GOD. What were some of the ideas you had about how that room would look? . . .

"There's a special prayer that's been written to go with this prayer experiment. Let's use it now; would someone like to read it for us? . . . Let's try to make this our prayer as we listen. . . .

**Dear God, so many people go through their whole lives and never stop to think that there are different values which can be at the center of these lives. We've had a look at 11 different philosophies of life. Please help us to choose the one which will make the most of the unknown number of years you've given us.**

(Proceed as above, collecting signs after each group has spoken so you can use them again. Each philosophy of life can be examined for its assets and weaknesses.)

(Try not to pass negative judgment unless something obviously needs correction—and in that case, be gentle; after all, who knows what "God's room" looks like?)

(If you can locate the music for room 11 on your record or tape, you might want to play it as soft background music for the prayer.)

(Notice that you haven't manipulated your students into saying, "Oh yes, by golly, the 11th room is the only one for me." That has to be their decision, not ours; some may want a life dedicated to making money.),

(Collect pencils.)

177

## — PART III —

"Now I'd like to invite you all to share your thinking on our super-prayer experiment with the rest of the class. I hope that each of you, or some of you, might be willing to tell us whether you think any of the philosophies of life we've been talking about (or some other) is the right one for you—and why. If you don't want to talk, maybe you'd be willing to raise your hand and be counted, if you think you have some definite idea on this topic.

"For instance, room one was devoted to status and position. How many think that's a good central value for life today? . . . ——————, would you be willing to tell us why you think this is true? . . .

*(if anyone raises his hand)*

*(Continue down the list; you can keep score on the board.)*

"Now, obviously you would expect me, as your religion teacher, to hope that many of you would want to put God at the center of your lives. And I do hope for that. Would anyone like to share his thinking on a God-centered life? . . .

*(A purposefully vague question to allow time for a witness talk—see Chapter 4—from you.)*

"You might have guessed that I'd pick the 11th philosophy of life, a life based on God, as my personal choice. I don't think I've ever told you why I feel this way, and if you don't mind listening I'd like to tell you now. . . .

*(Our kids assume, of course, that their religion teachers place God at the center of their lives. How often do we spell it out for them? Do we feel free to say how much we love him, how empty our lives would be without him? Feel free now, and speak to them as a fellow human rather than as a member of the establishment.)*

"To wrap up this superprayer experiment, which really gives you your wings as pray-ers, let's try together the simplest prayer of all. God is always with us and in us. St. Paul said, in fact, ". . . it is no longer I who live, but it is Christ who lives in me." Let's just be still, together, for a minute and soak ourselves in God's presence, like sponges in water or raisins in oatmeal or . . . ? Will you try this with me while our 'walking music' plays? . . .

"Thank you."

*(Gal 2: 20)*

*(Play opening of* Pictures at an Exhibition.*)*

**DATE TRIED:**                    **TIME:**                    **REPEAT?:**

**RESULTS:**

179

# chapter 9
# A POSTSCRIPT

Two currents are in the air these days, sending out their good vibrations to the religion classroom as well as to many other spots.

One is the charismatic renewal spoken of in Chapter 2, the Pentecostal movement which has spread rapidly among non-fundamentalist Christian churches in the past few years. If you're fortunate enough to have a prayer group of these Christians nearby, check it out, by all means. If not, you might read up on the Pentecostal experience; a good introduction is *The Pentecostal Movement in the Catholic Church* by Edward D. O'Connor, C.S.C. (Notre Dame: Ave Maria Press, 1971. $1.95). This renewal, one facet of the widespread rebirth of religious enthusiasm sometimes called "the Jesus Movement" or "The Jesus Revolution," centers around praise of God and—to use an old-fashioned spiritual expression—the indwelling of the Holy Spirit.

Most of us probably won't be quick to introduce the evangelistic tone of the charismatic renewal into our classrooms, at least not until the majority of our students are at ease with open prayer (oh, happy day!). How, then, can this movement color what we do as religious educators?

Well, those involved in the charismatic renewal pray differently than do old-line Christians. Whereas most of us were taught to ask God politely for favors and grace, expecting that somehow he would answer our prayers in proportion to our worthiness, the Pentecostal approach is to praise him exuberantly and pray with "expectant faith," faith that—since all is possible to the Lord—he will respond to the prayers of anyone with trust enough in him. Most of us have been conditioned to expect our reward after we're six feet under; the charismatic renewal teaches that we can all have the experience of life with God here on earth if we ask for it in faith. Jesus tells us (Mk 11: 24), "When you pray and ask for something, believe that you have received it, and everything will be given you." How many of us really believe him at his word?

Obviously, the religion teacher whose own prayer has the tone of trust and union and oneness described here will have more to bring to prayer experiments and his students than the teacher whose spiritual life is more juridic, less abandoned. For this reason, as well as several others, a thorough look at the charismatic renewal is almost a must for today's religious educator.

The second current "current" affecting our field is humanistic psychology. Those familiar with this branch of psychology, and with work being done in growth centers across the country, have already recognized its influence on this book.

Those religion teachers who haven't as yet discovered the many-pathed territory of the humanistic psychologists have a treat in store for them. So great is the importance of this field of study, and of its implications for education, that we could say teachers of all colorations have a responsibility to their students—and to themselves—to investigate it.

Basically (and this is a great simplification) the thinking of humanistic psychology is that man has tremendous potential, most of which is never developed, and that it's about time we did something about this. These "human potential people" want to help man grow physically, mentally, emotionally, socially, and—of special interest to us—spiritually. They do this through methods and research in a wide assortment of man-centered studies: physical fitness techniques, "growth games," prayer and meditation of all religions, educational methods and reform, parapsychology, mental health, alternative life styles, art and creativity, nutrition, and many, many other such areas.

The Association for Humanistic Psychology, formed in 1962, describes itself in its literature as encouraging attention "to topics . . . such as love, creativity, spontaneity, play, warmth, ego-transcendence, autonomy, responsibility, authenticity, meaning, transcendental experience (and) courage." Religion teachers will agree that these good things are also very much their concern. The *Journal of Humanistic Psychology* deals with this matter; information on both the *Journal* and the AHP can be obtained from headquarters at 416 Hoffman Avenue, San Francisco, California 94114.

A related journal, concerned with that fascinating area where religion and psychology interweave, is the *Journal of Transpersonal Psychology.* You might check your library for it or write to this journal at Box 4437, Stanford, California 94305. Transpersonal psychology delves into the so-called "altered states of consciousness," such as those brought on by meditation and mystical experiences, and, to quote the journal, ". . . essence, bliss, awe, wonder, self-actualization, ultimate meaning, oneness (and) cosmic awareness. . . ." Far out? Compared to what most of us in religion education have been doing, yes. Compared to what we should be conscious of if we hope to get our kids effervescent about God, no.

Two related recommendations: *A Catalog of the Ways People Grow* by Severin Peterson (New York: Ballantine Books, Inc., 1971. $1.65) is a comprehensive paperback of what's going on in the human potential field right now. An overview of the current scene, it will give teachers many leads for reading, thinking and programs of their own, all of which will eventually touch their students. You may not—almost surely will not—agree with all in this book, but it's an excellent summary of where people's heads are today.

Valuable also for us is a recent book on prayer which has roots in humanistic psychology: *God Is More Present Than You Think* by Robert Ochs, S.J. (New York: Paulist Press, 1970. 75 cents).

Fascinating is the interweaving of ideas from Eastern religions into the Christian framework in books like *Let's Start Praying Again* by Bernard Basset, S.J. (New York: Herder and Herder, 1972. $4.95).

Those of us who believe deep inside what we preach and teach, that each soul is infinitely precious and wonderful to God, can't afford to overlook the exciting (and very religious, in the broad sense of that word) research being done today on man and his potential. Our motto could well be this sampler verse:

"Let me come to you with wonder
At sensing God in your soul,
With my gifts of time and love and concern
That help you be yourself most whole."

**INDEX**

## INDEX OF CURRICULUM TIE-INS

As suggested earlier, prayer time can be—but doesn't have to be—connected to the subject matter of the lesson for the day. For those teachers who would like to hook up prayers to the themes of their lessons, here's an index of the more important curriculum tie-ins specifically touched on in different experiments. The numbers refer to prayer experiments, not to pages.

The following multipurpose experiments are flexible enough to be adapted to many topics and/or seasons of the Church calendar: 6, 9, 10, 11, 14, 21, 22, 23, 25, 42, 43, 45

# TEACHER'S NOTES

(NOTES)

(NOTES)